# We've Been Doing It All Wrong?

*Rethinking the Heart of Ownership*

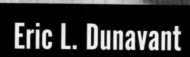

## Eric L. Dunavant

Cover Photos courtesy of mennoknight.files.wordpress and aussiescanners.com.au

Published by

**Burkhart** *Books*
www.BurkhartBooks.com
Bedford, Texas

# Endorsements

"Eric shares his personal life stewardship journey with disarming candor and refreshing transparency. His style invites you to take a path less traveled; a path that will produce a radical transformation for the better in every area of your life—if you dare to embrace it. His message is biblically-based and practically sound. If you want to upgrade the quality of your life and the effective stewardship of all God has entrusted to you, this book will definitely point you in the right direction!"

Jay Link—Author, Speaker, Life Stewardship Coach

"As the leader of a stewardship ministry at a large church, I was looking forward to reading *What If We've Been Doing It All Wrong*. After completing the book in one sitting, I was not disappointed! This is a book I highly recommend! I will be using it as a resource in my own financial ministry to help people along the same journey Eric followed in viewing money and possessions from a biblical perspective."

Dave Briggs—Director, Enrich Financial Ministry, Central Christian Church of Arizona

"Teaching on our stewardship of life, resources and the opportunities we have been given by God is not an easy task. Eric's new book is a great resource to further our personal efforts to be more Christ-like in the midst of our materialistic world. Through personal story telling and experience shaped by many years of client coaching, Eric has written a very informative and easy to digest book."

Gunnar Johnson—Author, Executive Pastor, Gateway Church, Southlake, Texas

"What we believe determines what we do. A simple yet profound truth! If we have the right beliefs, we'll generally do the right things. Eric challenges us to consider what we believe—what we believe about essential truths that shape our worldview and influence how we invest our time, talent and treasure. Eric's perspective will likely cause you to reframe some very basic beliefs; and, therefore, reform some of your present and future actions. In doing so, your life will be enriched ... both now and for eternity!"

Bill Williams—Former President of Generous Giving and Former CEO of National Christian Foundation

"Eric's book, *What If We've Been Doing It All Wrong*, is a compelling challenge to the standard approach to financial planning. His challenge to us as followers of Christ who are stewarding time, talent and treasure is to be recklessly faithful. In other words, he challenges my prevailing paradigm of being safe with my life and money. I think Eric's exhortation to live with reckless faithfulness is consistent with what Jesus invites me to in 'taking hold of the life that is truly life.' It was worth my time to read this book."

Todd Harper—Author, President of Generous Giving

"I am so pleased that my friend and colleague Eric Dunavant has written this book. I've spent over 50 years in the financial services world, and I know God's Word speaks authoritatively and transcendently to all financial planning and decision-making. Eric has captured the fundamental truth that your worldview drives all financial thinking and behavior. He communicates so well using personal examples based on his own experience and highly professional competency. I recommend this book to anyone who wants to take a thoughtful look at how money entrusted to us by our Lord is handled."

Ron Blue—Founding Director, Kingdom Advisors

"I've had the pleasure of knowing Eric and Angel and their kids now for several years. They inspire and challenge and bless me, and I'm certain the same will be true for you as you journey with Eric through these pages. One thing I know for sure is that what you will read here is an overflow of Eric's heart both for Jesus and for people. He cares deeply about the subject matter, and I admire him so much for that. This is not a "topic" for him, it's a calling. You'll feel that through the written words. My favorite part of this book is Eric's vulnerability and genuine spirit. He seeks to teach so that others may avoid his pain and mistakes. He seeks to affirm so that others may experience the rich blessings he has felt in obedience. This book has the opportunity to change you. To form you. To disrupt you. To bless you. Please let it. Let God move in and around you as you consider this important topic and the ways it impacts all of our lives."

Chris Field—Mercy Project, Founder and Executive Director

"Eric Dunavant has written an excellent book about a subject many followers of Christ neglect or misunderstand. Jesus taught how we use our (His) finances are of paramount importance. You will be blessed to hear the story of the Dunavant family and how understanding the true meaning of finances has made such a difference in their lives. This is an easy and enjoyable book that packs a punch. It will help you see how we have gotten it wrong and now how we can do it right."

Waylon Bailey—Senior Pastor, First Baptist Church,
Covington, Louisiana

# Dedication

First and foremost, I dedicate this book to my Lord and Savior Jesus Christ. This book came from Him; I am simply the vessel to convey the message.

To the best gift God ever gave to me, my bride, Angel Dunavant. Thank you for putting up with the mornings I left at 5:00 a.m. so I could get the writing time in. Thank you for all of the reading and editing. I love you this much " ".

# Acknowledgments

To my children, Clayton, Austen and Gracyn, thank you. There were some Saturday mornings and Sunday evenings you sacrificed to make this book happen. Your actions and spirit please me beyond measure.

Thank you to the pioneers of Christian Stewardship who came before. This book isn't anything new, it is simply a fresh perspective. I have had the honor to learn from the best.

A shout-out to Jon, Tim, Drew, Chad and Jerome who make up the band *Switchfoot*. Many hours were spent writing while you played in the background. You were crafting your 10th album while I was writing this book. On my journey, this book is "Where the Light Shines Through."

# Contents

# Introduction

Do you like to tell stories? Share information with others? Laugh, joke, even cry with friends? Do you have the best story ever to tell, but you realize in order for your audience to truly understand what really happened, you will have to go back to the very beginning—back to the part of the story which really seems like it has no impact on the end result, but it actually does? It makes all the difference in the world to lay the foundation!

That's what I need to do. I need to take you back to the beginning so you can understand the end. I hope you will be patient with me. I want you to see my journey— how I came to comprehend worldview as well as its impact on everything in my life—but first I need to go back to the starting point.

In the summer of 1996, I was a fifth-year senior at Texas A&M University. I had met Angel, my future wife, and was ready to graduate, but I had a couple of credits left to finish. One of the classes I needed to take was a class on world cultures. I didn't have any idea what to expect. I was excited to learn most of the class consisted of watching films and reading books, as opposed to a great deal of lectures. Naively I thought to myself, *"This should be easy."* What I didn't expect was how that class would introduce me to a concept I had never considered before—worldview.

Worldview is defined as "the overall perspective from which one sees and interprets the world" or as "a collection of beliefs about life and the universe held by an individual or a group."[1] The professor of that class didn't use the word "worldview" during the course, but as I've gotten older, I've realized the objective of the class was to challenge what I believed and why I believed it.

A little about me: I was raised in West Texas, in a small town outside of Lubbock. Most of my life was spent within a 300-mile radius of Lubbock, and everything I knew about the world centered on what I had learned from the people in that community. During that World Cultures class, my views were challenged. As I watched videos of people living in different environments, I was exposed to their traditions and what their culture said was acceptable. Some of the things I saw ranged from curious to intolerable based on the way my parents had raised our family. The teacher explained how in those cultures these behaviors were considered normal. Furthermore, if I disagreed with how these individuals were behaving, then I was narrow-minded.

Many of the videos and books I read caused me to question what I believed. This was the first time I had been exposed to the concept of having a worldview, and it took many years of study and the impact of strong spiritual influences on my life before I was able to reconcile what I experienced in that course.

**There are many different influences that can shape what I believe.**

However, that World Cultures class did help me. It helped me to realize there are many different influences that can shape what I believe. The same is true for everyone I interact with on a daily basis. If I don't understand how my worldview shapes me—the way I act and interact with those around me—then I open myself up to vulnerability and confusion.

Have you ever noticed your own worldview affecting what you think or how you observe something? I recently had an experience like this when discussing politics with a friend I've known since childhood. It struck me as odd because we were raised in the same small town and from what I could tell, our parents' outlook on life was very similar; however, as we got deeper into political viewpoints, it became obvious we were on opposite sides of the fence. How did that happen? How did this good friend who had a similar experience growing up, end up with a political position completely opposed to what I believe? Del Tackett is an author and speaker who created a series on Christian worldview called *The Truth Project*. He says, "Worldview is something much deeper than your personality or how you hold a golf club. It defines your beliefs about reality and your outlook on life."[2]

There had to be something deeper. I was slowly becoming aware I had my own personalized worldview. I was intrigued at how we all thought differently, and I wanted to learn more. I learned that there are actually two levels of worldview and once I understood this, things became a great deal clearer for me. Del Tackett refers to them as the formal and personal worldviews.[3]

A formal worldview is a group or ideal I subscribe to openly and obviously. This was easy for me to understand. I graduated from Texas A&M University; therefore, I have an Aggie worldview. I think Texas A&M is the best team to support in all sporting events. I can't imagine ever supporting anyone else. If A&M is playing sports, I have to be watching (or at least be frequently checking my phone). If anyone else is playing, I might be somewhat interested, but I also could be just as happy doing something else. My love for Texas A&M governs my formal worldview; however, if I spent time with someone else who graduated from Texas A&M, we might find sports is the only topic we agree upon. Formally, we both have an Aggie worldview, but it doesn't mean we both believe all the same things. Similarly, many Americans would say they are Christians, so therefore, they have a Christian worldview. This formal worldview may seem to unite us, but it doesn't really define what we truly believe. It only unites us on the surface.

You can contrast this with a personal worldview. This is how I truly view the world and how I act based on those beliefs. Each of us has a personal worldview, even if we do not understand or acknowledge it. Del Tackett said, "When someone says I am a Christian, therefore I have a Christian worldview, it may not necessarily be true, because what I believe formally may not be what I believe personally. In order to have a Christian worldview, it might require me to have a standard against which to measure what I'm choosing to use in my life."[4] Discovering and defining our personal worldview can take some soul searching.

I finally realized although my friend and I shared a formal worldview based on where we were raised, it didn't carry over in our personal worldviews. We had both gone off to college in different areas, and from our other conversations it became clear there were influences that shaped his thoughts and ideas differently than mine.

This led to even more questions in my mind. What was shaping *my* worldview? Was I even aware of the influences I was allowing in my life? Just a few years ago, I was at a Christian business conference. One of the speakers asked us to take time to consider who was shaping our worldview. With this one question, my spirit was broken. I started to realize how many outside influences I was allowing in my life that had nothing to do with my Christian worldview. My opinions and my outlook were not being shaped by what I knew to be true from the Scriptures. I was allowing others to shape what I believed.

**It was obvious the world had a plan to shape what I believed.**

I began to realize I wasn't paying any attention to what was shaping my personal worldview. I started to see influences in the television shows I watched, the music I listened to, the books I read and the people I hung out with. It was obvious the world had a plan to shape what I believed, and if I didn't come up with my own plan, I might end up on the wrong path. I knew formally I had a Christian worldview, but the majority of the influences in my life didn't come from sources that are based on biblical truth. I was relieved to find out I wasn't alone. The Barna Group is a market research firm specializing in studying the religious beliefs and behaviors of Americans. One of their more recent studies found only 19 percent of professing Christians actually live with a Christian or biblical worldview in their actions.[5] My relief quickly caused me to become unsettled as I realized for the number to be that small, there truly was a problem in the Christian community understanding what God wants us to believe.

It was such a conviction, I came to the realization that although I saw myself as having a formal Christian worldview, I wasn't living that out in my life personally. I was taking a little bit of truth from many different sources and creating my own gumbo of beliefs. As Del

Tackett says, "Living with a hodgepodge of unexamined beliefs makes lives purposeless and fragmented. On top of that, when our beliefs don't accurately represent reality, we end up acting in ways that hurt ourselves and our relationships."[6] I knew it was time for a change—a change that would be a bit radical and definitely unprecedented.

There are four times in Matthew where Jesus says to the Pharisees, *"Have you not read …?"*[7] Jesus was telling the Pharisees that all the knowledge they needed was in the scrolls they were to read. Personally, I knew I had not been reading the Scriptures the way I *could* or that I knew in my heart I *should*. It became clear my worldview was not as biblical or as Christian as I wanted to believe it was.

I began to hold up the truth of the Scriptures in many different areas of my life and began to realize I was compartmentalizing where I would allow God to work. I found it was easy for me to apply God's messages to raising my family or how I treat others, but His instructions did not end there. What became obvious to me was I was living my Christian worldview on Sundays, but unintentionally abandoning that worldview Monday through Friday. I traded in my biblical worldview Sunday night for a secular, temporal worldview. I was segmenting pieces of my life and had convinced myself there were areas where God's Word did not need to apply.

**… Most of the world around me encouraged me to leave God out of the picture.**

I slowly started to see there were two filters through which I was viewing life. One filter was determined by God's truth while the other filter blatantly left God out of the picture and was solely defined by man. I also realized it was very easy to live life without using God's filter. In fact, most of the world around me encouraged me to leave God out of the picture.

As I began the journey to actively change my worldview, I found it was very similar to going to the gym for the first time in several years. In 2011, I started doing Crossfit®. When I started out, I felt clumsy, I wasn't quite sure what to do, and a day or so after I finished, I hurt so bad I could hardly move. The more I came back, learned from the coaches and stayed consistent, it became easier and I became stronger. Today, I still get sore, but I know what to do and how to manage my recovery. I also have a passion for getting to the gym on a regular basis.

As I studied Scripture, it was much the same process. I began by feeling clumsy. I didn't know where to start reading, and so I sought counsel from those I trusted. When I was around people living a biblical worldview, they used some language that didn't make as much sense in the beginning, but over time became more familiar. I find the more time I spend studying and learning, the stronger my spirit becomes. There are times when certain scriptures will convict me in an area of my life, and I've learned how to manage those and put them to productive use in my walk. The more time I spend refreshing and renewing my mind with God's worldview, the more I want to be fed from it.

My journey to living my faith seven days a week was not without many new discoveries. As a person who spends much of his time in the financial world, I was surprised at how much a biblical worldview can affect the way I view finances, money and the economy. I knew the Bible had wisdom on how I should handle money, but I didn't realize where I placed God in light of those truths would be so important. I found the Bible contains 500 verses about prayer, a little less than 500 verses about faith and over 2,000 verses that speak on how to handle money and commerce. I also discovered Jesus spoke more on money and possessions than He did on heaven and hell combined!

## ... Applying God's Word to my faith and my business would cause me to change the way I work.

This book is a story of my journey. I began to realize applying God's Word to my faith and my business would cause me to change the way I work. What I ultimately discovered was a biblical worldview plus a true understanding of stewardship caused me to ask the question, "What if we've been doing it all wrong?"

If you will come, I would like to take you on this journey as well. As I looked deeper, I found different solutions to common financial questions. I also found a much deeper satisfaction and joy in my work. God's Word has been speaking for centuries on how we should manage His wealth. I pray we have the courage to listen. If we do, I believe we will experience everlasting peace only He provides.

# Chapter 1

# Understanding Worldview

## The only difference between you and I are the lenses through which we view the world ...

I've never worn glasses, but most of my family does. I've always been amazed when I hear people comment, "I didn't realize how bad I couldn't see until the doctor gave me new glasses." Having a worldview is much like wearing glasses. The lenses will determine what you see. Imagine you have spent your entire life looking at life with red-tinted lenses. If that were the case, then most likely, the color white in your world is more a shade of pink. You and I would probably have a hard time agreeing on the color of many items, especially those that are tinted red. The only difference between you and I are the lenses through which we view the world—our worldviews.

There are four primary areas of my worldview that have been transformed the most as I looked closer at biblical truth: creation, work, economics and understanding the true value of money. As I studied, I realized in these areas, I had bought into the world's way of thinking and left God out of the picture. It never was intentional, but the world had a plan to help me think without a mind towards God. As I began to unpack the differences of God's truth versus man's truth, I began to re-shape how I viewed the world. I think the element that most surprised me on this journey was how I had bought into the world's thinking without even realizing it. It began to frighten me when I realized without God's grace of revealing His truth to me, it would have been easy to stay blinded.

## CREATION

As I studied the idea of creation, I began to wrestle with the consequences of what I believed. In a biblical worldview, when I add God to creation, I realize creation has a purpose. Without His involvement, there is no created world, and we have no purpose. Is there a purpose if life just "happened"?

As I was growing up in West Texas and on into college, my science classes taught the earth evolved over millions of years. I was led to believe man evolved from some toxic goo and descended from the apes. In addition, because of the amount of time it took the earth to evolve, the earth needs to be protected because man can damage the earth.

I actually observed this view being communicated recently when my family and I were at the Museum of Natural History in New York City. There was a video on the history of the earth being shown on a loop at the beginning of an exhibit. The video ended with a comment that the most dangerous threat to our world is human beings. I was being admonished for existing because my existence is destroying and hurting the earth.

As I looked at Scripture, this idea stood in direct contrast to God's Word. Genesis begins with the account of God creating the heavens and the earth. I can see and observe an organized world around me that shows evidence of creation and not the chaos I would expect from random chance. Our family has had the opportunity to spend summer vacations in many beautiful parts of our country. When I'm in the mountains, I see God's creation. When I look at the stars on a clear night, I see the works of God's hand. I personally believe it takes much more faith to believe all of this came together as an accident than it does to believe in God the Creator. I think this idea is summed up best with what Paul says in Romans.

*For since the creation of the world God's invisible qualities—his eternal power and divine nature—have been clearly seen, being understood from what has been made, so that people are without excuse.*

Romans 1:20

One of the areas I see this conflict of worldviews played out is in the area of science. I love science. Our son, Clayton, has a periodic table of elements on the wall in his room. Our freezer, refrigerator and kitchen have been the home to many different experiments the kids have conducted over the years. However, without a creator, we have no need for God in science.

The scientific process is powerful and plays an important role in our society, but it seems to me we are beginning to come to a place of replacing God with science.

Science has given us some of the greatest revelations of our lifetime, and I look forward to what it brings in the future, but I think we also must acknowledge God gave us science to observe and see Him and His creation at work. Science, when studied and observed in light of a Creator, glorifies the Creator and His revelations. When science is god, it glorifies the one who makes the discovery and science itself.

## Science is *not* God; science *reveals* God.

What I now understand is science is *not* God; science *reveals* God. This may seem like a small point or idea, but what I found is that ideas have consequences. The belief we are here for only a short time without rhyme or reason to our existence extends to the other areas of worldview. Knowing we are "fearfully and wonderfully made"[8] should cause great joy.

## WORK

When I view the world with the belief God created me for a purpose, then the next logical conclusion is that my work has meaning. However, if my view is man simply evolved for no purpose, then he has no real value and his work is useless rather than productive.

*The Lord God took the man and put him in the Garden of Eden to work it and take care of it.*

Genesis 2:15

Even before sin entered the world, Adam was working and in the joy of the Lord fulfilling the calling God had given to him. This began to shape the knowledge I found in Scripture that work is worship and a calling; work is not punishment. It isn't something we *have* to do; work is something we were *created* to do.

Without God, the worldview seems to believe work is more painful labor than the worship we experience as believers. I imagine all of us know what the initials TGIF mean: "Thank God It's Friday." This represents a worldview that lives for leisure and not for work, yet I've also been guilty of uttering those words after a long week.

Under God's plan, we see the joy of work, but we also find work is required of us.

*Anyone who does not provide for their relatives, and especially for their own household, has denied the faith and is worse than an unbeliever.*

1 Timothy 5:8

This scripture seems to make it clear if we are not willing to work, it is as if we have denied our own faith. This scripture is in direct conflict with what I see today. Notice, this is not an issue of ability to work, but rather, it is an issue of willingness.

What I notice is that our culture seems to demean the value of certain people and their contributions, especially the poor. Since in a secular worldview man has no value, our government creates systems to support the poor. On the surface this seems like a good plan, but have we allowed it to go too far? T.M. Moore is an author and thought leader on Christianity in science and economics. He defines slavery as, "A system used to prop up a sector of the economy on which they have become dependent and allows them to maintain a comfortable lifestyle."[9]

Unfortunately, programs to support the poor often lead to a system in which the people feel they need to continuously be supported through government programs rather than trusting God for their daily bread. It is easy to understand that the more people are provided benefits and support, the more dependent they become on that support. Unfortunately, we are creating slaves to the system rather than providing solutions to help individuals improve upon where they are today.

## ... God created the earth for a purpose, and He created me for a purpose—to work.

As I read in the truth of God's Word, God created the earth for a purpose, and He created me for a purpose—to work. If this is true, then every person and their contribution is valuable, and we risk losing the contribution of those who are trapped in the government system. We seem to be curbing a desire to work God placed in us from the very beginning.

*Whatever you do, work at it with all your heart as working for the Lord, not for human masters since you know that you will receive an inheritance from the Lord as a reward. It is the Lord Christ you are serving.*
Colossians 3:23-24

I've found in my own life, I am not as obedient to this instruction as I would like. Too often, I get caught up in the distractions of the mundane; however, I do know what worshipful work looks and feels like. In fact, it is one of the greatest times of worship I have personally known. I have seen glimpses of this type of work when I volunteer or go on a mission trip. When I am working unto the Lord, I can feel the joy of the Holy Spirit and the work, no matter how hard, goes easily. This scripture is evidence to me God is inviting us to experience this every day.

## ECONOMICS

As I reconciled the idea God created the world for me to work in joyfully, I had to dive deeper. I am a "money man." I thrive on economics. I wanted to know more about what God said about economics and our internal desire to be productive. I know it is possible to be working and productive, but if I have no purpose, then I serve only myself. I knew in my heart this was not positive, but until I was able to observe this in action, I did not realize just how quickly things could go wrong. In reading the writings of T.M. Moore, I discovered three consequences of this man-centered worldview are alive and well today.

## THE FIRST CONSEQUENCE IS **GREED**.

To quote him: "People spend more than they should for things they don't really need, accruing debt that they can't really handle, leading to large-scale economic instability."[10] Wow, to me that seemed to be a definition of the last 15 to 20 years of our economy. I noticed everything I'm exposed to in advertising, music and even around my colleagues is about getting more than I already have. I think the famous song about not getting any satisfaction says it best. Rather than be content with where God has placed me, it becomes okay to borrow money or to extend myself beyond my current ability to try and find that satisfaction.

## THE SECOND CONSEQUENCE IS **EXPLOITATION**.

T. M. Moore states that, "Hoarding, price gouging, cartels and monopolies, bribes, price-fixing, and a wide range of scams and scandals can ensue when every man is seeking to do what is right in his own eyes."[11] Through working in the financial industry, I immediately thought of the 2001 bankruptcy of Enron and the more recent Ponzi schemes of Bernie Madoff and Allen Stanford. These scandals left many employees and investors penniless in their wake. I also realized the financial collapse of 2008 was driven by the exploitation of borrowers by banks and lenders. Exploitation seems to say that, "If all I want to do is what's important to me, then lying or cheating to get there doesn't really matter, especially if it makes me happy."

## THE THIRD AND FINAL CONSEQUENCE IS **IDOLATRY.**

T.M. Moore defines idolatry as, "Trusting in things and wealth to bring happiness and satisfaction in life."[12] I've always said I didn't want to sacrifice my family on the altar of success. As I've lived out my life, I've found this to be a delicate balance. Sometimes it would be easier to schedule an appointment or go to a meeting than it would to block out time for one of my kids' school performances. Early in my career, I even bought into the lie that, "If I could just get that next raise or promotion, then I would be happy." I quickly discovered how empty that pursuit was. When I devote my primary attention and energy to the acquisition and consumption of things, then I've made idols out of false gods that cannot deliver the meaning, happiness and peace I am seeking.

## A New Paradigm

What then, did God intend His economy to look like? As I studied, I found He created me to work in harmony with His creation. My striving and effort to outdo God were futile and chasing after the wind. God created the world to be responsive to my work. If I will be content and trust in God's perfect plan, then He has given me all I need. I observed this directly in scripture.

> *Then God said, "Let us make mankind in our image, in our likeness, so that they may rule over the fish in the sea and the birds in the sky, over the livestock and all the wild animals, and over all the creatures that move along the ground." So God created mankind in his own image, in the image of God he created them; male and female he created them. God blessed them and said to them, "Be fruitful and increase in number; fill the earth and subdue it. Rule over the fish in the sea and the birds in the sky and over every living creature that moves on the ground."*
>
> Genesis 1:26-28

As our world has moved from an agrarian economy to a service economy, it is often easy to forget God's role in our provision. Fortunately, I had the benefit of being raised in a family of farmers. My grandfather and his brothers were cotton farmers in West Texas. As they worked the land, they saw it produce abundance for them and their families.

---

**... It is often easy to forget God's role in our provision.**

---

Additionally, my father was a country veterinarian and my uncle worked on ranches. I was taught from a very young age to work hard, but I also observed the usefulness and productivity the livestock and working animals provided to man. Our family experienced daily reminders God had placed these animals in our lives for us to use to His glory.

> "Yet he has not left himself without testimony. He has shown kindness by giving you rain from heaven and crops in their seasons. He provides you with plenty of food and fills your heart with joy."
>
> Acts 14:17

This scripture paints a picture of a God Who created a world for me to use and that world would in turn be responsive to my work.

This view of our world and economy was a new paradigm for me. Rather than having to protect the earth from my actions, I see an earth and economic system God has created to serve me when I treat it responsibly. When I understood I had been created with a purpose, it actually decreased the pressure I felt to perform. God has created me to fulfill a specific purpose and rather than try to outrun His desires for my life, my role is to seek Him and live out that purpose. In doing that, God says He will *fill my heart with joy.*[13]

# THE TRUE VALUE OF MONEY

A temporal worldview says whatever makes us happy or works best for us and our situation will typically direct our money and our actions. T. M. Moore sums it up well when he states, "Without an eternal framework and revealed guidelines to direct (money), it quickly becomes a game of getting and spending, where it's every man for himself in figuring how and to what ends the money should change hands."[14]

Even in charitable giving there is no true satisfaction without God. The only end to giving in a temporal worldview is to glorify *me*. I acknowledge I feel good when I give, but am I making it a worship of self? Often, the more I give, the more recognition I find I need. It might come in the form of a plaque or a dinner, but the larger the gift, the larger the recognition I expect.

### ... I began to see money as a tool to glorify God.

As I studied the truth of Scripture, I observed that, "God gives us the ability to produce wealth,"[15] and that "everything in heaven and earth"[16] belongs to God. If both of those are true, then I own nothing, and I owe everything I have today to the God who gave me life. If I don't own anything, then the value of money changes completely. Rather than seeing money as a tool to be used to glorify *me*, I began to see money as a tool to glorify *God*.

The fulfillment of this is complete when I return back to Him a portion of what I receive. I can give my time and talents to others in service. I also can give back financially.

In the beginning and throughout Scripture, I found examples of returning portions of the gifts they received back to the Creator.

> *In the course of time Cain brought some of the fruits of the soil as an offering to the Lord. And Abel also brought an offering.*
>
> Genesis 4:3-4

We will discuss the heart of the offering and how it was received in a later chapter, but what I see is both men realized the value in bringing an offering.

The greatest challenge came to me when I realized God actually asked me to test Him in my financial giving.

> *"Bring the whole tithe into the storehouse, that there may be food in my house. Test me in this," says the Lord Almighty, "and see if I will not throw open the floodgates of heaven and pour out so much blessing that there will not be room enough to store it."*
>
> Malachi 3:10

God knows how important my money and finances are to me, but He also wants me to be able to experience the joy of Him in giving back.

Since I began my journey of understanding worldview, I haven't been able to look at the world in the same way. I would challenge you to ask yourself if you've been looking at the world from a true biblical worldview. The areas of creation, work, economics and value of money are just starting points for seeing the world through God's viewpoint. This has been a continuous journey for me, and I'm hopeful you will join me.

As I wrap up this chapter, I'd encourage you to look at the chart below where I've highlighted the difference between God's Wisdom in a biblical worldview vs. the temporal worldview I find standing in direct conflict. I'm going to unpack each one of these in later chapters, but I think it's important to take a look at the differences and see if you recognize places where you have been operating from temporal worldview and need to consider whether a biblical worldview more truly reflects what you value.

| BIBLICAL WORLDVIEW | TEMPORAL WORLDVIEW |
|---|---|
| God owns everything, and I want to know what He wants me to do with what He has entrusted to me (Psalm 24:1). | I made it, so it's all mine. |
| My ability to make wealth comes from God and not solely from my own hard work or intelligence (Deuteronomy 8:17–18). | I am the master of my own fate. |

| BIBLICAL WORLDVIEW | TEMPORAL WORLDVIEW |
|---|---|
| Poorly thought out and excessive inheritances can destroy the people I love most (Proverbs 20:21). | The more I pass on to my heirs, the better. |
| The best investment I can make is in The Kingdom (Matthew 6:19–21). | Building "my kingdom" is the first priority. |
| It is more blessed to give than to receive (Acts 20:35). | It is more blessed to keep than to give. |
| "True Life" comes from being generous (1 Timothy 6:17–19). | Getting rich and having more is my priority. |

What I have found in my own life is that changing my worldview has empowered me in my relationship with Christ. I feel I have more wisdom and more guidance as I make decisions based on His laws and His economy. In T. M. Moore's commentary, he says, "We must engage all commerce as stewards of a trust. God has given us gifts, resources, skills, and opportunities to be faithful in economic endeavor."[17] Over the next few chapters, we're going to spend time talking more about these worldviews. I believe you are in for a great adventure as we continue to uncover God's truth as it relates to retirement, inheritance, investing and giving. I have enjoyed God's revelations though the Scriptures and other biblical teachers, and I hope you'll begin to experience the same joy and freedom I have found by aligning my worldview with that of my Creator.

———————————

- How important is your worldview?

- Who have you let shape your current worldview?

- If God did not exist, how would this affect your purpose in life?

- What steps can you take to sharpen your worldview?

———————————

# Chapter 2

# Understanding Stewardship

A temporal worldview says, "I made it, so it's all mine."

A biblical worldview says, "God owns everything, and I want to know what He wants me to do with what He has entrusted to me."

*The earth is the Lord's and everything in it, the world and all who live in it.*

Psalm 24:1

At the end of the previous chapter, I quoted T.M. Moore who said, "We must engage all commerce as stewards of a trust. God has given us gifts, resources, skills and opportunities to be faithful in economic endeavor."[18] I think it is important that we have a good definition of stewardship, because I find it's a word that is typically only used in Christian circles. I know it's not a word I use in casual conversations.

As I was growing up in a small church in West Texas, I really thought stewardship had something to do with giving. Why did I think that? Well, when I looked in the church bulletin, the update on the collections was called the Stewardship Report. Anytime the church needed to have a fundraiser to build a new building or pay for a mission trip, they called it a Stewardship Campaign, and I always heard that people who gave regularly were considered good stewards. I never had any other reason to believe differently.

---

**... I had to experience a change in the way I think, the way I love and the way I live.**

---

Later, I began to grow in my faith and discovered I had an incomplete understanding of stewardship. I found stewardship took on a completely new meaning once I understood how it shapes everything in my life and not just my giving or finances. To truly understand stewardship, I had to experience a change in the way I think, the way I love and the way I live.

## Changing the Way I Think

How could changing my understanding of stewardship change the way I think? Let's start with the temporal worldview that says, "I made it, so it's all mine." Although I had grown up in the church, those thoughts rang true to me. I never really understood the concept that God owns everything.

To be transparent with you, when Angel and I were living in Arizona and had been married for only five or six years, the top priority of my life was to be wealthy. My mother died while I was in high school, and her illness led to my father filing bankruptcy before I graduated. These experiences shaped my beliefs that the only way to be secure was to have enough money to protect myself from repeating that tragedy.

I put much time and energy into reading books, listening to audios, and watching television programs to find business ideas. I spent many hours evaluating ways I could improve our financial situation. Everything I learned left me with a belief that it was my responsibility to build wealth, and if I just followed certain set actions and prioritized my goals then I would be able to achieve my ambition.

About this time, we were attending church in Arizona, and they offered a class on finances from a biblical perspective through Crown Ministries. At this point in my faith journey, I still had an incomplete understanding of God, but I thought the Scriptures might have the magic formula I was missing that would lead to my ultimate achievement of wealth. Boy, was I in for a surprise as the next thirteen weeks of the study would completely re-shape my views.

Each week of the class we were responsible for memorizing scripture before we arrived. Each scripture played an important role in the lesson, but it was the scripture of Week Two that would change me from that day forward. I've listed it below.

*Everything in the heavens and earth is yours, O Lord, and this is your kingdom. We adore you as being in control of everything. Riches and honor come from you alone, and you are the ruler of all mankind; your hand controls power and might, and it is at your discretion that men are made great and given strength.*

1 Chronicles 29:11-12 (TLB)

This scripture was so deep and packed with incredible wisdom. As I read through and internalized it, it really disrupted my world. I think it would be valuable to walk through each section and see if it has as profound an effect on you as it did me.

*Everything in the heavens and earth is yours, O Lord, and this is your kingdom. We adore you as being in control of everything.*

I had to confront the fact that everything belonged to God. *Everything* is a very strong word. I tried to find a loophole, but there was none. I also had to submit to the fact that this was His Kingdom and not mine. That was difficult as I had been ruling my own little kingdom for nearly 30 years, and I thought I was good at it. Not only did I have to give up control, but this scripture said I needed to adore Him for His control. At the end of the day, I was giving up my control and, in short, being told to be happy about it.

**... I was giving up my control and, in short, being told to be happy about it.**

38

*Riches and honor come from you alone and you are
the ruler of all mankind; your hand controls power
and might, and it is at your discretion that men are
made great and given strength.*

My life's ambition may have been to become rich,
but this scripture said riches and honor come from God
alone. In addition, He rules mankind and gets to decide
who is made great and given strength in the eyes of
man. I could set as many silly goals as I wanted, but only
He could control if I achieved them. How is someone
supposed to process this? For me, I had to come to a
place of total surrender.

This was where I realized perhaps I've simply
misunderstood the real meaning of stewardship.
DICTIONARY.COM defines a steward as, "a person
who manages another's property or financial affairs;
one who administers anything as the agent of another
or others."[19] One of the most influential authors, in my
understanding of stewardship, is Jay Link. He tells a story
of a retail store manager who helps to better illustrate
this position.

"Imagine that you have been hired to run a men's clothing store. The owner
gives you very specific instructions to open the store at 9:00 a.m. and close
the store at 7:00 p.m. He asks you to put the ties and slacks on sale and
vacuum the floors every evening before closing.

You've worked in the retail business for years. You know that no one shops
before 10:30 a.m. so you decide to open the store at 10:00 a.m. You also
know that most people stop shopping by 5:00 p.m. so you decide to close

at 6:00 p.m. It is almost springtime and no one is buying ties and slacks. Instead you decide the shorts and casual wear should be on sale. Finally, the store does not get a lot of traffic during the day and you believe the carpets look great. Therefore you decide to only vacuum every other day.

If you manage the store in this manner, how long will you be the manager?

Most likely, not very long!"[20]

If I am just the manager of God's stuff, then how well was I following His instructions for management? During the first week of the Crown study, we memorized Luke 16:11.

> *"So if you have not been trustworthy in handling worldly wealth, who will trust you with true riches?"*

I had to begin to ask if I was being trustworthy with what He had given to me.

For Angel and me, this caused a powerful shift in our lives. It also made me realize if all these scriptures were true, then stewardship doesn't have much to do with my giving. I may make giving decisions, but after I give the money away, that money is no longer mine to steward. Stewardship has much more to do with what God has me retain than it does with what God has me give. I had never considered that before.

Jay Link introduces three versions of a question that will help us to check our heart and motives as we live out our stewardship daily.[21]

What do I want to do with all my possessions?

What do I want to do with God's possessions?

What does God want me to do with His possessions?

I know in my heart question #3 is the right question to ask myself. I also know it's easy for me to acknowledge that God owns everything, but I want to be in control of the decisions. It's not as easy to stop and ask the owner what it is He wants to do.

---

### Submission is giving in but surrender is giving up.

---

The real change in my life came when I realized I have to not only submit to God's will but I had to surrender to His calling. Submission is giving in, but surrender is giving up. I had to surrender to God's control and desires for every area of my life. I remember at one point praying to God to better understand how to live out this surrender. We were on vacation in North Carolina, and I felt God saying to me, *"What if you never become wealthy or well known? Are you okay with that? Do you trust that I have a plan for your life and will you surrender to that plan no matter the outcome?"* It was then I began to understand what surrender looked like in my life. Although I had submitted to God, I had never surrendered my dream of being wealthy. I had to trust that God is the One making the decisions and know He has a perfect plan for my life. Surrender is a daily activity, but if I trust Him to take care of me, then I have all I need. I know surrender may sound difficult, but fortunately, we have a great example in Christ.

> *"For I did not speak on my own, but the Father who sent me commanded me to say all that I have spoken."*
> John 12:49

I would probably find myself in a whole lot less trouble if I followed the same example and let God guide my speech. Too many times I go forward with whatever is on my tongue without thinking how God might want me to respond.

I also find Jesus, in His darkest hour of prayer, realized the power of surrendering to the Father. In Matthew 26:39, He says, *"My Father, if it is possible, may this cup be taken from me. Yet not as I will, but as you will."* God has shown me over and over the more I surrender to Him, the greater the blessings I realize. He has continued to pour out His grace and blessing on my life, and the only change I can contribute is that I moved from submission to God to total surrender. I found I gained more by simply giving up.

**Once I began to think differently, I found that I began to love differently.**

God has continued to reshape my mind and my thinking as I better understand Him. Once I began to think differently, I found I began to love differently.

## Changing the Way I Love

Understanding stewardship has really had a profound impact on the way I love others. If I understand God owns everything, then I am free from the bondage of owning anything, and I find that my ability to love expands supernaturally.

A few years ago, we were visiting Angel's aunt when our niece backed a golf cart into Angel's Yukon. My first reaction was anger and frustration. Then I realized I really didn't own the Yukon, and if God wanted to put a dent in His car, then that was His issue. What was more important was the relationship with Angel's brother and his daughter. This circumstance actually brought us closer together. That could only happen out of love. Ultimately, God put a dent in His car because He needed to bring us all together.

In the middle of 2008, we experienced the worst stock market decline of my lifetime. It was a time of fear and frustration. Although I had followed all of the wisdom I could find in diversifying my investments, I was still experiencing losses. I finally had to reconcile myself to the understanding that if God wants the value of my investments to decline temporarily, that is His dominion.

*"Look at the birds of the air; they do not sow or reap or store away in barns, and yet your heavenly Father feeds them. Are you not much more valuable than they?"*

Matthew 6:26

The owner of heaven and earth knows what we need. I used this opportunity to serve and love others deeper. God used this time to help me learn more about contentment and His provision. Ultimately, by following a long-term strategy, I recovered from the losses I experienced. Additionally, many of my relationships were strengthened, and I was able to respond with actions that did not match what others expected from me during such a stressful time.

Does my attitude about material things change when I am motivated by love? Absolutely. Do you remember when you first met your spouse? I remember meeting Angel. She was on a date with someone else, and I tagged along. A few weeks later, I was able to ask her out on a date without the other guy around. God made it clear very early on that I had found my life partner in Angel. When I realized how much I loved her, money became no object. I wanted to buy her flowers. I wanted to buy her gifts. I looked for excuses to write her letters. When we are motivated by love, our desire to serve explodes.

There is an incredible account of this same love in scripture in Mark 14.

*While He [Jesus] was in Bethany, reclining at the table in the home of Simon the Leper, a woman came*

44

*with an alabaster jar of very expensive perfume made of pure nard. She broke the jar and poured the perfume on His head. Some of those present were saying indignantly to one another, "Why has this perfume been wasted? It could have been sold for more than a year's wages and the money given to the poor." And they rebuked her harshly. "Leave her alone," said Jesus. "Why are you bothering her? She has done a beautiful thing to me. The poor you will always have with you, and you can help them any time you want. But you will not always have me. She did what she could. She poured perfume on my body beforehand to prepare for my burial. Truly I tell you, wherever the gospel is preached throughout the world, what she has done will also be told, in memory of her."*

Mark 14:3-9

Did you read that clearly? She anointed Jesus with perfume worth more than a year's wages. She understood money was no object when you love.

As God changed the way I loved, I began to see things differently in the way I held onto them. If God made something for His Kingdom and chose to use my stewardship, I couldn't stop and ask why, I simply had to act. There's great joy in giving and ultimately the sacrifice is the reward.

I remember when we first opened our business. I didn't know what God would do, but I understood He would take care of me and my family. We had diligently saved enough money to last us for six months, which seemed reasonable considering the uncertainty of the future. Within the first week of opening the business, God made it clear we had saved too much money. He impressed on us if we maintained that reserve, this business would not have a story to tell of God's provision. Angel and I felt called to give away half of what we had saved. In man's economy, this decision would be hard, but in God's economy, it was easy. We wrote a check to several ministries and never looked back. The joy of the gift and the love we could share exceeded any concerns we might have had.

As my thoughts on stewardship expanded and my love for others grew more and more, I began to see a change in the way I lived. It didn't happen overnight, but the change was noticeable.

## Changing the Way I Live

Once we started to live under God's stewardship, we found it began to permeate many areas in our life we didn't expect. When we asked the question, "What does God want us to do with His stuff?" we found it changed the way we looked at everything in our life. When we started, we thought this would just be a change in our view of our possessions, but soon we realized God desired to have dominion over every area.

**How does God want me to steward my marriage and my kids?** This caused me to feel a greater responsibility and obligation not to take them for granted. The way I love and interact with my family is different when I realize how much of a treasure they are to God.

## We have to steward the decisions, but it's ultimately His responsibility to see us through.

**How do I manage the business He's given us?** I had to go to a place of total surrender of the ownership of the business. It's easy to surrender when things are going well, but what about when things are tight? That's been very freeing because every business problem becomes God's problem, not ours. We have to steward the decisions, but it's ultimately His responsibility to see us through.

**How do I care for the body He's entrusted to me?** Once we understood this concept better, Angel and I became much more focused on our health than we had before. Today, I do my best to exercise and eat well, not just because it's good for me, but because it is my response to stewarding the body God has given me. I'm in better health today because I'm obedient to God's stewardship, not because I prioritize fitness.

**How do I manage my time?** Time is our most valuable possession because each one of us has a finite amount to spend in our lifetime. We have to be diligent to make sure we are spending God's time wisely. On a day-to-day basis this may seem simple, but we found it was in leisure time we were the most vulnerable to wasting this commodity. As we considered God's desires here, we changed our choices of entertainment. We also limited the number of activities our kids could participate in because we saw the stress that over-commitment could cause. In addition, we quickly realized God's Word speaks clearly about a need for rest. We make it a point to find rest time in our week so we can be our best during our work time.

## ... Once I realized that I don't own anything, I experienced more freedom ...

I found that once I realized I don't own anything, I experienced more freedom in the way I thought, loved and lived than I had ever known before. I have a duty to follow His instructions, but I know if He is the One controlling the world, then I am in good care. As Jeremiah 29:11 states:

> *"For I know the plans I have for you," declares the Lord, "plans to prosper you and not to harm you, plans to give you hope and a future."*

Those plans sound much better than anything I could plan or imagine. Am I willing to wait patiently and find out how He wants me to steward the gifts I've been entrusted with?

---

- Why is it so important that we recognize God as the owner of everything?

- What would it be like if we were owners instead of God?

- Who truly benefits when we steward according to God's will?

---

# If We've Been Doing It All Wrong, How Can We Think Differently?

As I became clear on aligning my worldview and truly understanding stewardship, what I realized is both of these affect the way I interact in every single part of my life. I also realized they affect everything when it came to considering planning, investing and even giving. I don't know that I had ever considered how the way I believed would affect so many areas of my finances. As I reflected back on God's Word and what it said, I had to ask myself a simple question: "What if we've been doing it all wrong?" What if the traditional thoughts around planning for the future were coming from a temporal worldview and not a godly worldview? What would it look like if we used God's viewpoint to consider traditional planning and investing? I was both surprised and empowered by what I found.

# Chapter 3

# What If We've Been Doing It All Wrong in Planning for Us?

A temporal worldview says, "I am the master of my own fate."

A biblical worldview says, "My ability to make wealth comes from God and not solely from my own hard work or intelligence."

*You may say to yourself, "My power and strength and the strength of my hands have produced this wealth for me." But remember the Lord your God, for it is he who gives you the ability to produce wealth and so confirms his covenant which he swore to your ancestors as it is today.*

Deuteronomy 8:17-18

One of the biggest revelations I came across was the discovery that there are two CFOs in every family. Each family has a Chief Financial Officer and a Chief Family Officer. The Chief Financial Officer primarily wants to deal with numbers and financial outcomes while the Chief Family Officer is concerned about the impact each decision will make on their family and their relationships. In about 80% of families, the husband is the Chief Financial Officer and the wife is the Chief Family Officer. Each spouse often carries an element of each; however, one role is often dominant in making the decisions.

When focusing on the traditional view of planning, I knew the current process was broken, but it took some time to put my finger on what was off. Here are some issues I found were contributing to a broken system and, ultimately, to incomplete outcomes:

- A focus on financial outcomes only
- A focus on how, not why
- Beginning with a short-term "snapshot" view of the plan

The traditional planning process focuses primarily on financial outcomes. These are important, but really only speak to the concerns of the Financial Officer. Most Family Officers are more concerned with relationships among family and friends and the spiritual impact of the decisions to be made. Most find the process of engaging financial decisions boring, and the headache of having to deal with those details is often so frustrating they retreat from the process altogether.

Family Officers usually engage the process by asking "how" to do something. There are countless ways to help someone. The right "how" all depends on what you are trying to accomplish. The bigger issue is not "how" but "why" you want to do something. Why is this solution important? Most Financial Officers like "how" questions because they get the process over with more quickly. Family Officers realize if they understand "why" and take their time, they will probably end up with a better solution.

---

### I've never met anyone whose life was a snapshot; everyone's life is a movie.

---

Many Financial Officers would prefer to begin planning by offering a snapshot of their lives. "Here is some information about our family, our work, a copy of our balance sheet and our most recent tax return. What else could you need?" I've never met anyone whose life is a snapshot; everyone's life is a movie. The past affects the decisions you make today. Your vision for the future affects how you might do something. Financial Officers like the snapshot shortcut because it takes time to understand a situation better; however, most Family Officers appreciate taking the time to tell their story so everything is on the table before a decision is made.

The only way to gain understanding of what God is calling you to do is to spend some time together unpacking these issues. You have to dedicate a significant amount of time up front so both CFOs can share their perspective. Guided questions can help a couple get on the same page regarding the direction God has called them. This time helps both CFOs communicate together, and many times one of the partners learns something new about the other.

Not only does starting this way make sense, it's God's way of doing things. He puts couples together to complement one another. Why would you ever try to make a decision with "half" of your brain, yet many Financial Officers try to plan without involving the Family Officer.

There was a couple named Jerry and Mary. Every time there was a meeting about their finances, Jerry would come to the meetings alone. Despite several invitations, Mary wouldn't join him. When asked directly about this, Jerry would say, "Mary is just not interested in this stuff; she asked me to handle all of it." Once, when speaking to Mary, it was mentioned that her input was greatly missed in the decisions being made. She looked baffled and said, "Jerry told me I wouldn't want to be there because the conversation was centered on investments and numbers. I trust him to take care of those things."

This interaction is not uncommon and reveals the way it was being done wasn't helping her to focus on the areas of the planning that would get her attention. There are opportunities to have a clearer understanding of how she envisions their ideal lifestyle and help them make sure they have enough money to live comfortably until God calls them home. Such conversations typically draw in the Family Officer. It is essential to have a process that can gain the engagement of both CFOs and plan with a more complete picture.

When both CFOs get on the same page, they have to start with a critical question: "How much is enough for us?" Angel and I have found this one of the most difficult questions to answer for our family. Many other families wrestle with this question as well.

My worldview and beliefs around stewardship will affect how I arrive at this answer. From a stewardship standpoint, I have to go back to the Owner and find out how much He wants us to accumulate. I need to be in tune with what God wants me to live on and how much is enough for me and my family. I can't concern myself with anyone else. Through much prayer and study, we discovered there is a finish line for our lives. There is a point where we will have enough and anything beyond that number is outside of God's will.

## God is looking to save His people along all economic and income spectrums.

You must be careful with this decision because each person is responsible for their own stewardship. It is not your job to be the lifestyle police. Sometimes this is a challenge, because if you're not careful, you can cross over from helping someone be a steward to judging the decision they make in finding this answer for themselves. I found peace in this when I realized God is looking to save His people along all economic and income spectrums. The wealth families accumulate may allow them to witness to individuals in all areas of the social and economic spectrum.

You may know families who are multi-millionaires and own private jets. You may know families who live with very modest means. In each one of those cases, the heart of the person is more important than what they've accumulated. Each family has to respond to their role in stewarding what God has entrusted to their family.

When looking at long-term accumulation decisions, there are three areas that need to be addressed. The first is lifestyle, the second is debt and the third is retirement.

## Lifestyle

What are your dreams and desires for your lifestyle? Is there a second home you might want to build? Is there some travel you and your family might want to do? Or has God given you a dream or ambition of starting a business or a second career? These are all great questions of stewardship. Some couples purchase second homes not only for their pleasure, but also to allow families who are less fortunate or mission groups to use the home. Certain families use their travel for missions work or share their travel with extended family members who can't afford the trip on their own. Some people begin a second career that is more successful than their first because they found a way to pursue a joy and calling they didn't pursue the first time around. God has given each one of us dreams and visions for living out His calling and our lifestyle opportunities become an important part of how we live that out.

## God has given each one of us dreams and visions for living out His calling ...

The challenge we face is that a temporal worldview emphasizes the importance of getting rich and having more. I have found that each one of us struggles with balancing our call to stewardship against the desire to build bigger barns. What do I mean by "building bigger barns"? This is a reference to a parable Jesus told in Luke about a man who was accumulating a tremendous amount of crops. He had accumulated so much the crops would not fit in his existing barns. The man decided to tear down his current barns and build bigger barns to store all the grain he had accumulated.

> "Then he said, 'This is what I'll do. I will tear down my barns and build bigger ones, and there I will store my surplus grain. And I'll say to myself, "You have plenty of grain laid up for many years. Take life easy; eat, drink and be merry."' But God said to him, 'You fool! This very night your life will be demanded from you. Then who will get what you have prepared for yourself?'"
>
> Luke 12:18-20

Everywhere we look, the world tells us the importance of having more. The Forbes lists tell us who the richest people are, allowing us to compare our level of accumulation with theirs. Many times our self-esteem is tied up in how much we've piled up, and in the past, I've been guilty of trying to find meaning or happiness in what I've accumulated. Over the last several years many families have wrestled with placing their security in their Creator rather than in their wealth.

Have you noticed the media around us is selling fear? If we are not grounded in a biblical worldview, we would miss that not only does God hold us in His hands (Matthew 6:25–34), but the fact that we live in the richest nation at the richest time in history. Did you realize this? I initially found this fact hard to believe, but if you do a little research, you find out it is true. A family who makes more than $35,000.00 annually has an income that is higher than 99% percent of the rest of the world.[22]

If you are reading this book, there is a good chance you fall into that category. The question that begins to come to the surface is, "If I'm wealthier than 99% of the world, then why don't I have contentment?" I wrestled with this issue myself in 2001 when Angel and I were living in Mesa, Arizona, and both were working full-time jobs. I'd spent a significant amount of time during our first five years of marriage trying to come up with business ideas and investments that could ultimately make us rich. I discovered the pursuit of that goal made me miserable.

This was the time period when we took the 13-week course from *Crown Financial* on handling your money from a biblical perspective. (This course will keep coming up throughout this book because the teaching changed our lives completely.)[23] The very first class was on contentment. It reinforced the concept God has us exactly where He needs us today. Sometimes He is using our circumstances to teach us something and other times He is using our circumstances to teach others something, but no matter what, rather than trying to pursue some grand dream, I learned I needed to be content with where God had placed us for that time. If I could be content where I was, it was up to God to direct my steps.

Once I chose to be content with where God had placed me, He started blessing us more than I could ever have imagined.

In Philippians, Paul shares the secret to contentment:

*I am not saying this because I am in need, for I have learned to be content whatever the circumstances. I know what it is to be in need, and I know what it is to have plenty. I have learned the secret of being content in any and every situation, whether well fed or hungry, whether living in plenty or in want. I can do all this through Him who gives me strength.*

Philippians 4:11-13

**The secret to contentment is only found in a personal relationship with Jesus Christ.**

What was Paul's secret to contentment? It's certainly not material possessions as this letter was written from prison. Our material circumstances and possessions are not the secret to contentment. I love the way the scriptures work together when taken in context. Notice verse 13 which has often been used as a life verse for athletes or others facing a temporary hardship. Paul is saying the secret to contentment is only found in a personal relationship with Jesus Christ. Contentment in life does not come from what you have or what you don't have. It comes from **Who** has you.

## Debt

The second issue to consider with longer term savings is debt reduction. Many families wrestle with debt. People will quickly agree that reducing their short-term debt—credit cards and such—is a good idea. However, when it comes to long-term debt—homes and cars— most struggle with the idea this should be aggressively paid off. Have you ever caught yourself comparing the interest rate of a note versus the potential long-term investment rate you could earn if the funds were invested. If this were a world made up only of simple math, I think these decisions would be easier; however, even in math, I realize investment returns are not predictable, so the exercise does not always hold an easy answer.

I've also found great wisdom in comments from Christian financial author and business owner, Ron Blue. In his book, *Master Your Money*, he says, "Two spiritual dangers of borrowing money exist. First, borrowing always presumes upon the future and second, borrowing may deny God an opportunity to work. In James 4:16, presuming upon the future is called 'arrogance.' In many cases, when we borrow the money to fund one item, be it for the purpose of a new car, a television, a new home, a vacation, or whatever, we are putting the lender in the place of God. Who needs God to provide for us if someone will lend to us?"[24]

We also forget the world we live in is a spiritual world and our struggle is against spiritual forces.

*The rich rule over the poor, and the borrower is slave to the lender.*

Proverbs 22:7

Do we ever consider we are putting ourselves into the bondage of slavery when we borrow money? Angel and I have had the privilege of teaching financial classes based on biblical principles in which the first emphasis is on getting out of debt. In many instances, we witnessed God blessing families who made the commitment to reduce or eliminate their debt load. I watched families get an unexpected bonus. I've seen people get a raise or promotion. All of these things happened when they made a move to change their focus to getting out of debt. At first I thought it was a coincidence, but then I realized there must be something bigger going on. I realized once God can see a family committed to handling their finances from His perspective, then just like any good father, He wants to reward that commitment.

We have personally experienced the joy of getting out of debt as well as walking beside other families as they became debt-free. I don't believe I've ever seen a similar experience of happiness in someone's investment returns. Here are common quotes from those families:

*"I can't explain it, but the car just drives different now that it's paid for."*

*"Now that the house is paid off, we went in the backyard and walked around the grass in our bare feet. It felt better than it has ever felt before. It's like nothing I can explain."*

I believe I can explain it. I believe you are feeling the joy of your Father as you align His worldview with yours.

Please understand I am not completely against borrowing money. There are times when it makes sense (such as using borrowing leverage to buy real estate or a business); however, I have noticed in our culture, it is easier to turn to borrowing instead of turning to God to provide. Debt can sometimes be a tool, but you should proceed with caution. As I've mentioned, my personal life story is born out of borrowing gone wrong.

## Retirement

The last issue of focus is retirement. This is one of the areas where people usually have the most questions. It's also one of the areas where I see the biggest misunderstanding from a worldview standpoint. In the United States and around the world, we seem to have created this vision of retirement that I can't find reflected in the Scriptures. There seems to be an idea when we reach age 65, we should leave a productive lifestyle and move to a life of leisure and pleasure focused on ourselves. I don't find everyone believes this, but I do find it is a prevalent communication from our culture.

---

## The concept of retiring at 65 is relatively new ...

Have you ever caught yourself asking the question, "How early can I retire?" I've wrestled with this myself because part of me thinks it would be a lot of fun. However, the question I couldn't answer was, "What would I do if I retired?" The concept of retiring at 65 is relatively new, and as I mentioned, everywhere I look in the Scriptures, I don't see a reference to retirement or long periods of leisure.

Most historians credit German Chancellor Otto Von Bismark for introducing the concept of a pension at 65 years of age in 1889. During this time, there was a political issue where Marxists were threatening to take control of Europe. To hold them off and win the approval of his countrymen, the Chancellor offered to pay a pension to any nonworking German over the age of 65. The piece that worked in his favor was hardly anyone lived to be 65 at that time. With that act, he set the arbitrary world standard for the year at which retirement would begin.[25]

Retirement then made its way from Europe to the United States when we changed from a farming community to an industrial community. As long as farming was our primary occupation, most men would work as long as their health would allow them. When they got older, they might cut their hours or give the more physically demanding chores to their sons or their hired workers. "In 1880 when half of Americans worked on a farm, 78 percent of American men worked past the age of 65."[26]

As we moved into the factories, the new concept of retirement began to take hold for a couple of reasons. One, as the workers aged, they were less productive and these factories were all about productivity. Second, as the older workers continued to work, it created greater unemployment among the younger workers. The Great Depression made the situation even worse. The factory owners realized the best way to get the older people to stop working was to pay them enough to stop working. A Californian, Frances Townsend, initiated a popular movement by proposing mandatory retirement at age 60. In exchange, the government would pay pensions of up to $200.00 a month—an amount equivalent at the time to a full salary for a middle income worker. President Franklin D. Roosevelt then proposed the Social Security Act of 1935 which made workers pay for their own retirement income.

From a biblical worldview, we need to reframe the question. Instead of thinking of retiring to a life of leisure, we need to be in tune with what God is calling us to do in this latter part of our life. Jay Link is an author and one of the authorities on biblical stewardship. He has provided my favorite definition of retirement. "Retire-ment is where you take off the old tires and put on new ones and keep right on rolling."[27] How would you re-imagine the second half of your life with this perspective? One family used this time in their lives to become more active volunteering with their church and in the community. They found they had the time, and energy, to serve and pour into the lives of younger families. They also were able to be more involved in the lives of their grandchildren. It doesn't have to be a completely new career, but as I will discuss in the chapters on eternal investing, there is great joy in giving of yourself.

Before I finish this chapter, I have one more area I want to visit as we talk about building a plan for lifestyle, debt and retirement. One of the hardest parts of building a plan is developing a strategy for the future while balancing the concept of trusting God. What if God's will includes temporary detours or other instructions? We don't want to be so focused on the plan we miss hearing the voice of God.

What do you do when you deal with a job change? Many families have saved a significant sum in retirement and other assets. While traditional planning would focus primarily on the long-term and preserving the assets in investments, sometimes the answer isn't so cut and dry.

Each case is unique, but in every situation, the first question you must ask is, "God, what do You want us to do with what You have entrusted to us?" Some families are led to downsize a home. Some are called to take a temporary part-time job. Sometimes God's direction is to withdraw some of the retirement savings to live on. Rather than relying on one "traditional" answer, each family must seek God's will.

I've had to learn to hold my own retirement assets and savings loosely. I know God wants me to plan for the future and take care of my family, but at the same time, I want to be obedient to calls when He might need me to deploy that money in another direction. One of the greatest experiences Angel and I have ever had of trusting God happened when we opened our business. As I mentioned in the last chapter, God made it clear to both of us we had saved too much money. He was calling us to give it away so He could be glorified. In a temporal worldview, this made no sense. I don't have the space in this book to recount the blessings, but the only way we could experience them was through complete obedience.

When it comes to creating a plan, I think our ultimate direction comes from Jesus.

*"But don't begin until you count the cost. For who would begin construction of a building without first calculating the cost to see if there is enough money to finish it."*

Luke 14:28 (NLT)

We need to start by understanding what it will take to reach our goals and objectives. However, at the end of the day, we need to realize it is our stewardship of God's assets, and we need to be willing to be obedient to His instructions, even if they might vary from the original plan we put in place. I want to be open to the fact that sometimes He may call us to do things that don't make sense in a temporal worldview.

- Why is it important to have a plan?

- What are the advantages of understanding the WHY behind your plan?

- Has God called you to set any financial finish lines in your accumulation?

# Chapter 4

# What If We've Been Doing It All Wrong in Planning for Our Heirs?

A temporal worldview says, "The more I pass on to my heirs, the better."

A biblical worldview says, "Poorly thought out and excessive inheritances can destroy the people I love most."

*An inheritance claimed too soon will not be blessed at the end.*

Proverbs 20:21

Once a family can settle on "How much is enough for us?" the focus turns to asking the next question. "How much is enough for our heirs?" The temporal worldview says, "The more I pass on to my heirs, the better." Put another way, you leave your children as much as possible, no matter the consequences. Most families wrestle with this issue more than any other.

---

**A biblical worldview would not simply leave an inheritance without regard for the consequences, good or bad.**

---

I've observed that the goal of most estate plans is to maximize the inheritance to the kids. I've actually heard attorneys say, "The first goal is to help the family pay as little tax as possible. After that, we want to get everything else to the children." In a temporal worldview, the number one concern is the impact on the estate rather than the impact on the recipient of the inheritance. I agree it is important to minimize the taxes, but a biblical worldview would not simply leave an inheritance without regard for the consequences, good or bad.

At the risk of sounding like a broken record, the only question I can ask as a steward is, "God, how much should I leave to my children and grandchildren?" I don't know if this question is all that easy to answer. In order to determine the right solution, there are a number of decisions each family must consider:

Why should we leave an inheritance?
What is the purpose of the inheritance?
What should we leave for an inheritance?
How much should we leave for an inheritance?
When should we leave an inheritance?

It is in the area of inheritance we find the two CFOs—the Chief Financial Officer and the Chief Family Officer—often have the biggest departure in agreement. It is important that both partners work together and use a biblical worldview to come to consensus in this area.

## Why Should We Leave An Inheritance?

It is helpful to begin with the question, "Why should we leave an inheritance?" Many people begin by responding with scripture. Proverbs 13:22 (NKJV) says:

*A good man leaves an inheritance for his children's children.*

I believe this scripture is wise, but we also need to make sure we take it in context.

Randy Alcorn is a Christian author of many books on wealth and giving. I appreciate his thoughts on this area of scripture. He says, "In Old Testament times, passing on ownership of the land to children and grandchildren was vital. Most were too poor to buy land. With no inheritance they could end up enslaved or unable to care for their parents and grandparents, who normally lived on the property with them until they died. Today in America, however, the situation is very different. Inheritances are usually windfalls coming to people who live separately from their parents, have their own careers, are financially independent, and already have more than they need. They have dependable sources of income generated by their own work, skills, saving, and investing. Having it will simply mean increasing their standard of living, sometimes dramatically."[28]

The best way to unpack this question begins with another question. "What is your view of an inheritance?" There are two views most parents typically hold. Many Family Officers believe an inheritance is an inherent right or an obligation that must be fulfilled because your children were born into your family. Many Financial Officers believe an inheritance is an unearned privilege or a choice. This viewpoint acknowledges the desire to leave an inheritance but sees it more of a blessing opportunity than an obligation to fulfill.

Tim and Gloria, a couple from the Midwest, wrestled with this very issue. Gloria felt strongly that they had an obligation to leave the children money through an inheritance. Tim wrestled with this idea because he watched a childhood friend suffer through life because he had inherited a trust fund. The biggest challenge was helping them come to an agreement on this issue.

I believe the reason this question is so difficult is we typically have a positive view of what an inheritance can do. It's not in our nature to think about the negative effects an inheritance could cause. However, we have to realize by giving anything to our children and grandchildren, we are effectively taking away something at the same time.

Jay Link tells the story of a young teen getting a new BMW for his first car. Although this sounds great on the surface, Jay points out some great lessons I think we often miss. "If you give your son a brand new BMW convertible for his first car, you will take away ... what? This dad has likely taken away his son's ability to ever be content with any less of a car. He certainly has taken from his son the opportunity to experience the satisfaction of working hard and methodically saving up to buy his first car and appreciating what it really costs in time and money to own a car like this. Admittedly, this father was giving his son a very generous gift. In so doing, however, he was likely taking away several experiences that would be far more valuable to his son in the years ahead than the car."[29]

With an inheritance, we also can unintentionally take away our children's struggles.

> *Consider it pure joy, my brothers and sisters, whenever you face trials of many kinds, because you know that the testing of your faith produces perseverance. Let perseverance finish its work so that you may be mature and complete, not lacking anything.*
>
> James 1:2–4

If mom and dad have the ability to keep their children from failing, they are effectively denying their children the opportunity to learn how to overcome life's struggles. We see this lived out in the life of the caterpillar. When the caterpillar makes its cocoon, it is the struggle of escaping the cocoon that allows the butterfly to fly. If you disrupt this process, the butterfly will never fly and will actually die.

---

## ... It is the struggle of escaping the cocoon that allows the butterfly to fly.

---

Once Tim and Gloria looked at these ideas with a fresh biblical worldview, they concluded there was an amount of inheritance they believed was an inherent right and a portion that was an unearned privilege. Different families will arrive at different conclusions but only after a great deal of prayer and discussion. This question, however, is only one of the questions that can help a family walk in wisdom towards solving this dilemma.

## What Is The Purpose Of An Inheritance?

As we understand why we are leaving an inheritance, we can then ask what purpose the inheritance might serve. Most families have not put a lot of thought into this question. To keep it simple, there are two purposes for most inheritances. An inheritance can serve the purpose of providing an opportunity or it can provide a certain lifestyle.

The Chief Financial Officer is typically drawn to inheritances that can provide opportunities while the Chief Family Officer often sees more of the lifestyle needs. Most families find agreement when they discuss the various opportunities they may want to help their heirs achieve.

Let's consider how a couple in Texas, Bob and Janet, addressed this in their lives. As they were setting their goals in this area, a lot of Bob's thoughts (the Financial Officer) were in the opportunity category, while Janet (the Family Officer) was more focused on lifestyle needs the inheritance could address. As typically happens, they agreed on many of the items in the opportunity category; however, they spent a considerable amount of time discussing what a lifestyle inheritance might look like.

The first opportunity Bob and Janet wanted to provide was to make sure they could fund an education for their children and grandchildren. They also agreed they wanted to help their kids get a good start by providing some money for an emergency fund and a down payment on their first home. Bob was an entrepreneur, and he wanted to set aside some funds to help his children if they decided to start a business.

## Lifestyle inheritances typically have the most unintended consequences.

Lifestyle inheritances typically have the most unintended consequences and therefore require the most prayerful attention. Some situations favor leaving a lifestyle inheritance, such as when you have a special needs child who will need support throughout their lifetime. However, many times, the decisions in this area require special attention.

Janet had raised her children as a stay-at-home mom. She and Bob were considering providing an income to each of their children so the mom in the family wouldn't have to work. Initially this seemed like a good idea, but it led to a discussion of the consequences. How much income would they provide? Was there an amount that might allow the wife to live independent of her husband and possibly set up a lack of unity in the marriage because the spouses weren't dependent on each other? Would the husbands feel as if Bob and Janet had limited their ability to lead their household?

Bob and Janet had a daughter, Bethany, who was working in a mission capacity. They were considering providing some excess income so Bethany wouldn't have to worry about raising support every year. Would this deny Bethany some personal growth as she raised her own support and had to trust in God to meet her needs?

Lastly, Bob and Janet owned a lake house the family enjoyed on the weekends. They felt strongly they wanted it to go to the kids. The first thing was to ask the kids if they would want it. This may seem like a strange request, but some families have found themselves creating plans to pass on a property only to find out the kids didn't want it. Bob and Janet's kids did say they wanted the property, but they didn't have any idea how they would be able to pay for the ongoing maintenance it would require. This insight led Bob and Janet to make additional provisions in their lifestyle inheritance plans to be sure the family could maintain the home after they both passed.

None of these decisions are easy, and oftentimes there are compromises that need to take place. Sitting down and having a discussion around these questions helps you to be enlightened on the best purposes for the inheritance. The responsibility of making sure the inheritance ultimately accomplishes your wishes without sacrificing the opportunities and experiences that shape life is a delicate balance.

## What Should We Leave For An Inheritance?

The question, "What should we leave for an inheritance?" seems puzzling. If the only worldview you have is temporal, then every idea that comes to mind is financial or tangible in nature. In Ecclesiastes 7:11–12, Solomon, the richest man to ever live says:

*"Wisdom, like an inheritance, is a good thing and benefits those who see the sun. Wisdom is a shelter as money is a shelter, but the advantage of knowledge is this: Wisdom preserves those who have it."*

Similarly, author Ron Blue has said, "Wealth never creates wisdom. Wisdom may create wealth. If you pass wisdom to your children, you probably can pass wealth to them. If they have enough wisdom, then they may not need your wealth."[30] Taken together, it seems that leaving wisdom is much more important than anything else I might leave to my family.

---

### "Wealth never creates wisdom."

---

How do we leave wisdom? We can do that by spending time with our children and grandchildren. We forget we have a wealth of life experiences and stories that can help them better understand how to live a fruitful life.

In Deuteronomy, God gives us a great example of how to put this into practice.

> *Love God, your God, with your whole heart: love him with all that's in you, love him with all you've got! Write these commandments that I've given you today on your hearts. Get them inside of you and then get them inside your children. Talk about them wherever you are, sitting at home or walking in the street; talk about them from the time you get up in the morning to when you fall into bed at night.*
>
> Deuteronomy 6:5–7 (MSG)

In Chapter 7 on "Eternal Investing," I will talk about how experiencing giving together can create memories and opportunities to share wisdom while you live life.

If the goal is to leave wisdom, is there any way to measure how well you are doing? You can separate the family capital into three areas: spiritual, relational and financial. When measured against specific maturity markers, you can begin to see areas of achievement and areas for improvement.

How can you measure maturity in these areas? You can start by thinking about each heir and asking good questions. Typically, no one is perfect, and no one is completely deficient, but if you consider each area on a scale, you can begin to identify trends for each individual. Here is a sample of a tool created by Mitchell Baris, Carla Garrity, Carol and John Warnick, and adapted by Jay Link to reflect a biblical worldview.[31]

On a scale of 1–10 (1 is low – 10 is high), please rate each of your heirs based upon your perception of their current level of maturity using the following maturity markers:

### Spiritual Maturity Markers (Relationship with Faith)

#1  Actively growing in their faith
#2  Developing virtuous character
#3  Actively serving others

### Relational Maturity Markers (Relationship with Self)

#4  Taking responsibility for his/her actions and proactively seeking correction
#5  Controlling his/her anger, frustration, disappointment and stress appropriately
#6  Regularly avoiding chronic problematic and self-destructive behavior

### Relational Maturity Markers (Relationship with Others)

#7  Developing and maintaining healthy and meaningful long-term relationships with friends and family
#8  Treating other people with respect and dignity
#9  Making personal sacrifices for the benefit of others

### Financial Maturity Markers (Relationship with Money)

#10  Living financially independent of parents
#11  Exercising consumptive self-control in spending
#12  Actively engaged in joyful generosity in giving

Heir's name _____

#1____ #2 ____ #3 ____ #4 ____ #5 ____ #6 ____

#7 ____ #8 ____ #9 ____ #10 ____ #11 ____ #12 ____


Heir's name _____

#1____ #2 ____ #3 ____ #4 ____ #5 ____ #6 ____

#7 ____ #8 ____ #9 ____ #10 ____ #11 ____ #12 ____


Most families find that working through this exercise helps them to see where there are opportunities to sow into their heirs' lives further. Just as you would expect, the age of the person being measured will affect their maturity, but it is still helpful to know where they stand and where the greatest upside opportunities exist. Ultimately, it comes down to the thought that what you are accomplishing in your living room has a much greater effect on the impact you leave than anything that could ever be done in a lawyer's conference room.

## How Much Should We Leave For An Inheritance?

The question of, "How much should we leave for an inheritance?" typically never gets asked in a temporal worldview. Why? The reason is simple: I love my children and want to bless them as much as possible. If that is true, then in equal shares I leave them whatever is left over.

---

## ... The idea of equality is relatively new.

---

Creating an equal inheritance is an item many families wrestle with. It is interesting to note that the idea of equality is relatively new. In the Old Testament, the guideline was to leave an inheritance only to sons; firstborn sons were entitled to a double portion.[32] Only if the family had no sons were the daughters entitled to any inheritance.[33] I don't believe this instruction stands for us today, but I use it to show the context that Scripture did not consider inheritance an issue of equality.

In Jesus' Parable of the Talents in Matthew 25, we find stewardship and discipline are determinants of financial blessing.[34] In this parable, the owner left one of the servants with five talents (a significant amount of money), one with two talents, and one with one talent. Not only did they each start with a different amount, but he rewarded each of them differently.

Ron Blue calls this idea the *Uniqueness Principle: Love your children equally, and as such, treat them uniquely.* "I believe that a parent should consider differences in children—differences due to age, gender, temperament, their demonstrated ability to handle money, their spiritual commitment, their spiritual maturity, their known or unknown marriage partners, and their children. It is a parent's and grandparent's responsibility to entrust God's resources to children only if they have demonstrated the ability to handle those resources in a manner that would be pleasing to Him who is the owner of all."[35]

Both CFOs will wrestle with this idea initially. There was a couple, Victor and Sara, who were initially resistant to the idea of inequality. The oldest of their children was a successful attorney and was financially independent. Their daughter was recently divorced and raising two young children. As they thought through the stewardship of this inheritance, it became clear that the needs of their children were quite different, and therefore, the amount of inheritance should be unique. They discovered this was not an issue of needing to treat each of their children equally, but uniquely.

Additionally, when one child suffers with an addiction or other destructive lifestyles, there are specific considerations that have to be weighed. After prayer and counsel, many families agree that treating a child equally, in this circumstance, would do more harm than good.

The key element in any of these decisions is open communication. Victor and Sara made a point to discuss this decision with their oldest and found that he was in agreement that his sister needed specific help that wasn't a need for his family. This open discussion relieved the parents of any guilt and kept family unity.

**... Clear communication can help heal relationships over time.**

If one of your heirs is demonstrating less maturity, a decision to plan based on uniqueness rather than equality may provide an opportunity to pass on more wisdom or allow the heir to correct the deficiency. First and foremost, seek God's plan in these decisions. When hard choices need to be made, it is always easier to discuss them while you are still here to provide context to your heirs on why you made certain inheritance choices. They may not like it, but clear communication can help heal relationships over time.

As wealth increases, there is also a need to turn your attention to the possibility of limiting the total amount of inheritance you leave. As I stated earlier, we typically ignore the consequences excess access to wealth may create. In her book, *The Golden Ghetto*, Jessie H. O'Neill lays out what she calls the bitter fruits of excess inheritance.[36] They are very real and should not be neglected when making this decision.

The first bitter fruit is **a lack of motivation to work**. There was a family where a grandfather had left a trust of substantial size to each of his grandchildren. One grandson, Mike, was reaching his senior year of high school and his grades and performance in school were disappointing to his parents. When they challenged him to finish strong, he stated, "What does it matter what grades I get? When I turn 21, I get the trust Grandfather left for me, and I'll have enough money to be set for the rest of my life." I can't image the grandfather's intention was to take any motivation away from his grandson, but it was an unintended consequence.

In some cases, the bitter fruit is **a lack of perseverance**. This typically happens because there are no consequences in failure. One couple, Phillip and Ruth, discovered this pattern in their son as they were reviewing the amount of inheritance they wanted to leave. They reflected and realized they had given money to their son several times to help him start businesses. Unfortunately, when the businesses would get difficult, the son simply abandoned them rather than stick it out because he knew if they didn't work out, his parents would be there to provide more funds for the next idea.

Excess inheritance can also cause problems in relationships and lead to self-worth struggles. Many children of affluence never know if their friends are with them because of who they are or because of what they have. This can often lead to confusion and frustration where they don't know if the relationships they have are authentic. Some families spend an incredible amount of money and energy trying to protect their children "just in case" their marriages fail. Although the pain and possibility of divorce is real, these efforts often create a lack of trust and put a strain on the relationships within the family.

The last bitter fruit is **a poor understanding and management of finances**. Phillip and Ruth also had to wrestle with this when they realized they had done a poor job educating their children on handling finances. Phillip and Ruth found the path of least resistance was to take care of everything. As their children got into adulthood, they struggled with understanding how to manage it all. When they realized their mistake, they worked to speak wisdom into their children, but it was an uphill battle because they hadn't been educated from a younger age.

## When Should We Leave Our Heirs An Inheritance?

Most inheritance plans that are developed begin once you die. Unfortunately most professionals don't ask families to think about *when* they should focus on leaving an inheritance. As life expectancies increase, we are observing many parents living into their nineties. In these plans, most children wouldn't receive their inheritance until they were sixty or seventy years old. With a new perspective, most parents agree the time their children have their greatest financial need is during their mid-twenties through their early forties. At this age, they are starting careers and families and often make decisions based on financial trade-offs.

### ... Give gifts during your lifetime

One way to find out if the inheritance is accomplishing what you hoped, is to give gifts during your lifetime. Through these gifts, you can observe how they manage the gift and you can actively pass along wisdom as the opportunities arise. Additionally, you can watch them enjoy the inheritance at the same time you strengthen your relationships. These observations will also allow you to monitor their maturity and make more clear decisions about any future inheritances you may have in mind.

Answering the question of "How much is enough for our heirs?" is not so simple. Once you take the time to seek clarity and wisdom from God on how to steward this decision, it has the opportunity to create unity and harmony among both CFOs. Our heavenly Father loves us more than we love our own children and wants the best for us.

> *Trust in the Lord with all your heart and lean not on your own understanding; in all your ways submit to him, and he will make your paths straight.*
> Proverbs 3:5–6

- Do you lean more towards inheritance being an inherent right or an unearned privilege?

- What are the pros and cons of leaving your heirs a financial inheritance?

- How would you like to impact your heirs' lives?

# Chapter 5

# What If Our Financial Investing Is Temporary?

A temporal worldview says, "Building my 'kingdom' is the first priority."

A biblical worldview says, "The best investment I can make is in The Kingdom."

*"Do not store up for yourselves treasures on earth, where moths and vermin destroy, and where thieves break in and steal. But store up for yourselves treasures in heaven, where moths and vermin do not destroy, and where thieves do not break in and steal. For where your treasure is, there your heart will be also."*

Matthew 6:19-21

When I began my career, it was at one of the most unique times in investing history, right before the peak of the tech bubble in 1999.

I remember the euphoria of investors during this time. In case you have forgotten or never knew, in the late 90's, you had to try to *not* make money in the stock markets. There were investments that would go up 50%–75% quickly and everyone thought they were brilliant investors. I actually overheard a checkout clerk at our local grocery store give advice to a customer on a "hot stock tip." By the middle of 2000, the bottom had dropped out.

---

## Many people—myself included—replaced our hope in God with hope in our stock portfolios.

---

As I reflect back, I realize there was a lot of arrogance during this time period. Many people—myself included—replaced our hope in God with hope in our stock portfolios. When the bear market of 2000 continued through 2003, many people abandoned stock investing. Things got better from 2004 through 2007, but then the bear market of 2008 shattered the hopes of many others.

These experiences reinforce the need to understand everything we have here on earth is temporal. It will eventually all burn up. As the old hymn says, "This world is not my home, I'm just a passin' through. My treasures are laid up somewhere beyond the blue."[37] The last 20 years have been quite volatile with four periods of stock market losses that totaled at least 19% each time.[38] Surprisingly, it is not all doom and gloom.[39] During those years, despite the volatility, large company stock investments have still realized an annual return of over 8% per year.[40]

Many people have lost confidence in investing. The last 20 years have had many ups and downs, and as I thought about biblical worldview and my life, I wondered what God's Word might say about the way I look at long-term investing and the stock market. In Chapter 4, we mentioned the Parable of the Talents in Matthew 25. I think there is an incredible amount of wisdom in this parable for us to consider as we manage these temporal treasures God has entrusted to us.

*"For it will be like a man going on a journey, who called his servants and entrusted to them his property. To one he gave five talents, to another two, to another one, to each according to his ability. Then he went away. He who had received the five talents went at once and traded with them, and he made five talents more. So also he who had the two talents made two talents more. But he who had received the one talent went and dug in the ground and hid his master's money. Now after a long time the master of those servants came and settled accounts with them. And he who had received the five talents came forward, bringing five talents more, saying, 'Master, you delivered to me five talents; here I have made five talents more.' His master said to him, 'Well done, good and faithful servant. You have been faithful over a little; I will set you over much. Enter into the joy of your master.' And he also who had the two talents came forward, saying, 'Master, you delivered to me two talents; here I have made two talents more.' His master said to him, 'Well done, good and faithful servant. You have been faithful over a little; I will set you over much. Enter into the joy of your master.' He*

*also who had received the one talent came forward, saying, 'Master, I knew you to be a hard man, reaping where you did not sow, and gathering where you scattered no seed, so I was afraid, and I went and hid your talent in the ground. Here you have what is yours.' But his master answered him, 'You wicked and slothful servant! You knew that I reap where I have not sown and gather where I scattered no seed? Then you ought to have invested my money with the bankers, and at my coming I should have received what was my own with interest. So take the talent from him and give it to him who has the ten talents. For to everyone who has will more be given, and he will have an abundance. But from the one who has not, even what he has will be taken away. And cast the worthless servant into the outer darkness. In that place there will be weeping and gnashing of teeth.' "*

Matthew 25:14–30 (ESV)

There is so much wisdom in this parable I think it would be valuable to go through the passage verse by verse and see how it applies.

*"For it will be like a man going on a journey, who called his servants and entrusted to them his property."*

As we established in the chapter on Understanding Stewardship, we don't own anything. I often need a gentle reminder I am simply a steward. I am managing what God has entrusted to me until He returns, even when

I invest. Colossians 3:17 provides profound wisdom for considering my approach.

> *And whatever you do, whether in word or deed, do it* ***ALL*** *in the name of the Lord Jesus, giving thanks to God the Father through Him (emphasis added).*
>
> Colossians 3:17

If all I do is to be done in the name of the Lord Jesus, I began to ask myself something I hadn't considered before. "Are there certain investments I shouldn't own based on God's standards?"

---

### I am managing what God has entrusted to me until He returns ...

---

As I was studying scripture in this pursuit, I was led to Deuteronomy 23:18. It says: *"You must not bring the earnings of a female prostitute or of a male prostitute into the house of the Lord your God to pay any vow, because the Lord your God detests both."* I knew immoral actions were not acceptable to God, but this scripture shows **money made from immoral activity** is detestable to God. If God owns everything, including the earnings, then perhaps I should take a closer look at how I am investing His money.

I found this was not an easy task. I had never considered if any of the investments I owned might be companies that were participating in acts that are detestable to God. I also didn't know if there were any resources available that could help me take a closer look from a biblical perspective at how a company was making or using their profits.

Over time, I found two great resources that are leading the way in helping Christians discover how companies are deriving their profits. One is *eVALUEator®*, and the other is the *Biblically Responsible Investing Institute*.[41] With these tools in hand, I began digging a little deeper into certain companies I had seen in many portfolios.

The first was a company known for making baby hygiene products. I've used their shampoo on my own children. Between my children, nieces, nephews and working in the church nursery, I've powdered many bottoms with their baby powder. As I looked at research, I found this company also makes drugs that are abortifacients which prevent fertilized eggs from being implanted or cause the premature delivery of a fertilized egg. They also use fetal stem cells for their research. This discovery was an unpleasant surprise!

The next company I studied was a company that has done a great job of making technology cool. They don't have the cheapest products, but they have convinced everyone they are the best. I was saddened as I dug deeper into the company. What I discovered is this company allows many applications in their online store which promote violence, profanity and sexually explicit material. There have also been instances where they have restricted Christian applications from being available. In addition, they have also spoken out strongly and provided financial support in favor of lifestyles that challenge a biblical worldview of family.

If these two companies were not appropriate, I began to wonder if there was anything I could invest in. *eVALUEator®* has done a great deal of research in this area. They found there are over 10,000 publicly traded companies that are deemed large enough for prudent investment selection. Based on the scoring they have conducted, approximately 9,300 of those investments do not have any violations.[42] What I did find was that the larger a company is, the more influence you find the world has over its practices. The S&P 500 is a proxy for large company investments and roughly 250 companies listed on the S&P 500 are clean according to information from *eVALUEator®*. Knowing I still had 9,300 companies to choose from encouraged me that investing with my virtues is possible.

In addition to owning individual stocks, I knew that I could also own mutual funds in order to have greater diversification. I quickly found there were many mutual funds that classified themselves as "Biblically Responsible Investing." I was encouraged that I might have found a shortcut in some of my research. Unfortunately, that was not the case. It seemed each company had a different criteria for determining what stocks might be appropriate and what stocks might be unacceptable to own. There did not seem to be an industry standard.

---

**... How a company uses their profits is just as important as how they make their profit.**

---

Many of the biblically responsible investments use a screening which states they will not own investments that make a profit from actions considered objectionable. On the surface this sounds good; however, I found that many of them were not concerned with how the company uses their profits. My conviction is that how a company uses their profits is just as important as how they make their profit. Let me explain how this might look from a practical standpoint. There is a large company that makes a profit selling lumber and other construction materials. For some, this investment is acceptable because they do not make a profit violating any Christian virtues. However, if you dig deeper, you discover this specific company takes a stance against traditional family values and has made significant contributions to causes that are not aligned with a biblical worldview. I was convicted that a company that used their profits in this manner should also be avoided.

---

**To the best of my ability, I attempt to avoid all immorality in my investing.**

---

There are some good mutual fund investments that follow these more specific criteria, but you have to do your homework.

*I will be careful to lead a blameless life—when will you come to me? I will conduct the affairs of my house with a blameless heart. I will not look with approval on anything that is vile. I hate what faithless people do; I will have no part in it. The perverse of heart shall be far from me; I will have nothing to do with what is evil.*

Psalm 101:2–4

To the best of my ability, I attempt to avoid all immorality in my investing.

Any time someone looks at investments, the question of performance is close at hand. The Parable of the Talents makes it clear that performance is an important aspect of investing. I began to ask myself some more questions.

- If investing with my virtues caused me to gain a higher performance, would I choose to do it?

  - I found this an easy question to answer: **Yes.**

- If investing with my virtues caused me to get a similar performance to secular investing, would I choose to do it?

  - Again, this answer was easier to come by: **Yes.**

- If investing with my virtues caused me to get a slightly lower performance, would I still choose to invest that way?
  - I admit, this question causes some struggle. If I honor God with my investments, do I trust His provision? At the end of the day, my answer was: **Yes.**

Fortunately, the last question does not appear to be an issue. The Christian Investment Forum and Stewardship

Partners are two organizations who have done research that shows there is very little difference in performance between investments that screen for virtues-based investing versus those that do no screening.[43]

I had one nagging question that remained. "Am I being a hypocrite?" If I discovered that Apple had violations and I did not want to own their stock, can I still own an iPhone? I am not seeking legalism or guilt. I just want to honor God as best as I can.

I was able to settle this issue for myself when I considered the thought through the lens of ownership versus use. When I purchase a product, I choose how it can be used. If I purchase an iPhone, I can then use it to witness to others, I can read scripture, I can even listen to worship music; or I can access gambling sites on the Internet, I can look at pornography, or I could use social media to disparage others. I have personal control over how that product is used. When I own stock in a company, I profit from their actions and have very little control over how those actions are carried out. If a company I own takes a stance against what I believe in, and I profit from that, I was convicted that it would not please God. This struggle did lead me to look at my day-to-day life and seek out opportunities when possible to avoid using companies that violate my virtues.

In my own life, I find this specific stewardship question is as difficult as others. I encourage you to pray and discover how God would have you act based on this new understanding.

In the next section of the parable, God demonstrates how He chooses His stewards. God rewards us based on our ability. He has an expectation for how we manage what He has entrusted to us. He also loves us enough that He gives us an opportunity to demonstrate our stewardship back to Him.

> *"To one he gave five talents, to another two, to another one, to each according to his ability. Then he went away."*

Have you noticed that there are certain families who seem to be favored over others when it comes to the way God blesses their investments? There appears to be one trait these families share. They are focused on a long-term plan.

In Luke 14:28, Jesus confirms this when He says, *"Suppose one of you wants to build a tower. Won't you first sit down and estimate the cost to see if you have enough money to complete it?"* When investors are focused on specific goals that are based off of a longer term plan, they typically realize better outcomes.

Consider Ron and Stacy who started by building a plan based on God's calling for their life. Every investment decision they make is driven by the plan they created. They have been through market ups and downs, but having a plan has helped them to make rational, rather than emotional, decisions even in the face of uncertainty.

## God favors those who take the time to plan.

In contrast, families without a plan focus primarily on the short-term. There are families who insist on building an investment strategy without considering the long-term goals and plan. I have seen instances where those families fail because the only thing they have to focus on is the markets and their performance. Without a longer term perspective, they let the short-term fluctuations and temporary fear move them out of investments, often to their detriment. God favors those who take the time to plan.

The plan is important, but so are the results. The next portion of the passage focuses specifically on the outcome that each servant achieved.

*"He who had received the five talents went at once and traded with them, and he made five talents more. So also he who had the two talents made two talents more. But he who had received the one talent went and dug in the ground and hid his master's money. Now after a long time the master of those servants came and settled accounts with them. And he who had received the five talents came forward, bringing five talents more, saying, 'Master, you delivered to me five talents; here I have made five talents more.' His master said to him, 'Well done, good and faithful servant. You have been faithful over a little; I will set you over much. Enter into the joy of your master.' And he also who had the two talents came forward, saying, 'Master, you delivered to me two talents; here I have made two talents more.' His master said to him, 'Well done, good and faithful servant. You have been faithful over a little; I will set you over much. Enter into the joy of your master.'"*

Early on, I marveled at the ability of the two servants who doubled their money. Notice the master came back "after a long time." This information is critical to understanding what happened. Have you ever wondered how they realized such incredible returns? Although the scripture does not give us a specific time frame, it does provide a frame of reference to understand how these returns might be possible. If the master was gone for a ten-year period, the servant would need a return of approximately 7.2% per year; over seven years he would need a return of approximately 10.4% per year.

Do any investments we have access to today provide this type of return, historically? The returns that are needed have actually been achieved through large and small company stock investments. Over the last 80 years, small company stocks have provided annualized returns of over 12% per year. Large companies have provided over 10% per year, while bonds have realized an annualized return of less than 6% percent per year.[44] (When you shorten the time period down to 20 years, you continue to see this large discrepancy between the performance of stocks and bonds.) I think it is important to begin with the idea all stock investing is designed to be held for a long time.

Many families have been convinced stocks are risky and bonds are safe; however, that does not seem to be what the results tell us. In the numbers above, small company investments have provided double the annual return of bonds over longer periods of time. If you receive double the return, that doesn't seem to equate to risk. There is, however, a disconnect. There are three factors that contribute to most people underestimating the potential of stock market investing.

The first factor that contributes to underestimating stock performance is how the investment industry has confused us with their unique language. The words we use in our everyday lives matter. The word "risk" is often used when helping someone make investment decisions. Most investment professionals start by asking a prospective client to fill out a Risk Tolerance Questionnaire. It finally hit me that they've been using the wrong word.

## The words we use in our everyday lives matter.

DICTIONARY.COM defines risk as: "exposure to the chance of injury or loss, a hazard or dangerous chance."[45] In my life, the areas where I see risk lead to a chance of permanent loss. For example, I buy homeowners' insurance to cover the risk of our house burning down or being damaged in a natural disaster. Without insurance, I would have to cover that cost myself and depending on the damage, that could be quite sizable or next to impossible. If risk means I might never be able to use that item again, I want to be very careful how I manage it. If a financial advisor wants me to fill out a Risk Tolerance Profile, then there must be risk in investing. This is money for my future; I don't want to lose it forever.

If we look at the last 80 years of stock returns, we find significant average annual increases. Why then do we come to the assumption that stocks are risky? The answer lies in looking closer at the history of investing and how that history influences what we own.

In 1952, a young economist by the name of Harry Markowitz wrote a theory called "Modern Portfolio Theory."[46] This theory would go on to change the investment landscape forever. One of the ideas presented in the Modern Portfolio Theory is the concept of diversification, which has helped many investors balance their investments. One of the consequences of Modern Portfolio Theory is the fact that Mr. Markowitz effectively changed the definition of "volatility" to "risk" as it pertains to investing.

Volatility is defined as: "tending to fluctuate sharply and regularly."[47] Stock investing is very volatile. There are years when stock markets have lost more than 50% and years when they have made more than 50%.[48] The primary reason small company stocks provide double the average annual return of bonds over the last 80 years is because of the unpredictability of the stock returns from year to year. If you need access to your money during the next five years, it would be unwise to invest that money in stocks because that investment has much higher short-term volatility. However, if you have a "long time" to invest, stock investing has historically provided better potential returns than bonds or other instruments.[49]

In 1990, Harry Markowitz was awarded the Nobel Prize in Economics for his theory.[50] With this award, the investment industry married the definitions of risk and volatility together. Instead of asking how much volatility someone might tolerate in order to potentially gain greater return, they are asked how much risk they want. Most people are left making incorrect assumptions about how to invest their money because they are unable to differentiate the definition of investment risk from risk in their day-to-day lives.

The second factor that contributes to underestimating stock performance is having an improper expectation of performance. History shows we are unable to time the stock markets; however, I've found that a logical understanding of volatility doesn't keep us from wanting to try to control the unexpected. A bear market is defined as a loss of 20% or more.[51] If we look back at the last seven bear markets in the S&P 500, we find we experience this type of volatility approximately every five years.[52] Additionally, on average, the market has dropped 14% somewhere during the year almost every year since 1980 and yet 75% of those years ended positive.[53]

What is difficult is that four of the last seven bear markets happened in less than four months.[54] You can't avoid something that can happen that quickly. And just as the losses are unpredictable, so are the gains. During the last bear market in 2011, we experienced the majority of the loss in four months and recovered from those losses within four months.[55]

One of the most well-known money managers of the last decade is Peter Lynch of Fidelity Investments. He said, "Far more money has been lost by investors preparing for corrections, or trying to anticipate corrections, than has been lost in the corrections themselves."[56] Those who try to time the market typically do worse than if they simply rode out the volatility.

---

## The cost of long-term investing is sitting through the temporary declines as they come along.

---

Although these downturns are not pleasant, the only way to get higher returns is to be willing to experience greater volatility. Trying to suppress volatility also suppresses the long-term performance of the investment. Stocks have historically provided the highest returns, but if the volatility is more than you can handle, you shouldn't expect to be able to get the reward of higher returns. The cost of long-term investing is sitting through the temporary declines as they come along. As a bit of perspective, the first of the seven bear markets we have been discussing began in 1980 with the S&P 500 at 110. As we began 2016, the S&P 500 traded around 1900.[57] Seven bear markets have come and gone and still the average annual return is a little over eight percent return per year before adding in the dividends.[58]

The third factor that contributes to underestimating stock performance is recognizing the importance of diversification. As much as Markowitz created a disadvantage for investors by changing the definition of risk, he did them a great service when he encouraged diversification. What we find through Scripture is that King Solomon was teaching diversification thousands of years before Harry Markowitz.

*Invest in seven ventures, yes in eight; you do not know what disaster may come upon the land.*

Ecclesiastes 11:2

A biblical worldview emphasizes having investments in many broadly diversified categories such as large companies, small companies, international companies, commodities, real estate, etc.

Why should we diversify? First and foremost, there is no way to predict which investment categories will do well from year to year, or as King Solomon said, "You do not know what disaster may come upon the land." There are many resources which show the performance year over year for various investment categories. These resources show the performance of each category is highly unpredictable.[59] Diversification can potentially help make up for this high level of unpredictability by owning a piece of each area of these markets.

Unfortunately, many investors don't like the idea of diversification. The human tendency is to look at what has done well recently and believe that trend will continue. In 1999, many investors made large profits by holding only technology companies. Unfortunately, they chose not to diversify their investments, and many of those same investors lost 75% of their accumulated value because of the decline in technology stocks from 2000–2003. Unfortunately, there's no statistical evidence for the persistence of performance.[60] Just because something did well last year has no bearing on how it will perform this year. Solomon's wisdom is just as valuable today as it was thousands of years ago.

The first two servants seemed to have a good understanding of how these principles work. The third servant, however, was afraid, he was gripped by fear and the consequences were great.

> *"He also who had received the one talent came forward, saying, 'Master, I knew you to be a hard man, reaping where you did not sow, and gathering where you scattered no seed, so I was afraid, and I went and hid your talent in the ground. Here you have what is yours.' But his master answered him, 'You wicked and slothful servant! You knew that I reap where I have not sown and gather where I scattered no seed? Then you ought to have invested my money with the bankers, and at my coming I should have received what was my own with interest. So take the talent from him and give it to him who has the ten talents. For to everyone who has will more be given, and he will have an abundance. But from the one who has not, even what he has will be taken away. And cast the worthless servant into the outer darkness. In that place there will be weeping and gnashing of teeth.'"*

I was struck by the reaction of this third servant. How many times have I let fear keep me from reaching my potential? The wicked servant hid his talent because he was afraid. It seems that the goal of modern day media is to keep us fearful and concerned about what is happening in the short-term rather than encouraging a long-term perspective. As the options for consuming media have broadened, it seems media has become more sensationalized. Every time I turn to a news source, there is some new crisis. When I stopped to think about it, I realized that most media is driven by advertising. Advertisers can't sell their products if I'm not paying attention. Additionally, I pay better attention when I am frightened or anxious.

---

## ... I realized that most media is driven by advertising.

---

Angel and I saw this firsthand when we were evacuated for a hurricane (an uneventful one after Katrina). We kept the television tuned into news on the weather constantly. In truth, from minute to minute, there wasn't anything to report. However, the weatherman did a great job of creating an environment of fear which kept us watching.

In addition, our temporal nature is to focus on what's happening today and to expect that exact same pattern to continue into the future. This is known as Recency Bias. After living through Hurricane Katrina, we were more fearful of the hurricanes for the several years that followed. In the years following the economic collapse of 2008, many people kept expecting the next calamity to occur and because of this sold their long-term investments at the bottom of the market. The media helped to continue this thinking and had many people believing, "This time is different." By 2013, the market, as measured by the S&P 500, had returned to its previous high set in 2007, and many investors had missed out on the recovery because they let fear keep them from staying with their long-term investments.[61]

Throughout history we see that cycles are inevitable. Why should we expect today to be any different? There are periods of strong growth and periods of contraction, but over time the trend of the great companies in the US and throughout the world have been positive.

These cycles come and go, but I've found the greatest ally in creating fear in investing is the belief that the economy and the stock markets are somehow correlated. How many expert economists come on the TV or write a paper for the news trying to express how they see things turning out? Whether we realize it or not, they are wrong more than they are correct. I love the quote of John Galbraith, who served in John F. Kennedy's White House. He said, "The only function of economic forecasting is to make astrology look respectable."[62]

Historically, I find most of what I'm fearful about is related to government decisions. What I fail to remember is investing involves owning individual companies, not economies. The great companies of America and the world learn how to work around the madness of governments. Sure, there are periods when economics and business are correlated, such as 2000 or 2008, but over the long-term, the majority of businesses learn how to innovate and improve their profitability. This allows investors to potentially receive better long-term performance.

## ... Many investors allow short-term fear to interfere with their long-term decision-making.

The emotion of fear goes so far as to affect our behavior, often to our detriment. There is good research that shows behavior is one of the greatest determinants of long-term investment performance. DALBAR research kept up with the performance of investors over the last several decades. They found the average investor over the last 20 years has averaged 2.5% a year, only slightly better than inflation. During that same 20-year period, every traditional investment class performed better, including Large Company US Stocks which averaged 9.9% a year.[63] Why such a discrepancy? Because many investors allow short-term fear to interfere with their long-term decision-making.

Ultimately, Jesus gave the best investment advice:

*"So do not worry, saying 'What shall we eat?' or 'What shall we drink?' or 'What shall we wear?' For the pagans run after all these things, and your heavenly Father knows that you need them. But seek first His kingdom and His righteousness, and all these things will be given to you as well. Therefore do not worry about tomorrow, for tomorrow will worry about itself. Each day has enough trouble of its own."*
Matthew 6:31–34

If we can trust God with our eternity, I believe we can trust Him to take care of us while we are on this side of heaven.

Our goal in our investing should be to honor God. The real question is: Do we trust God to bless our efforts if we follow His principles? When volatility or uncertainty comes, is our trust in God or our investments? If it all belongs to Him and we follow His desire, do we have the right to be anxious if He loses money? The concept may seem difficult at first, but it is the worldview that will help us to honor God, have the proper perspective and one day hear: *Well done, good and faithful servant.*

* Do I trust God to bless my efforts if I follow His principles?

* When volatility comes, is my trust in God or my investments?

* If it all belongs to God and I invest according to God's principles, do I have the right to be anxious if His investments lose money?

## Chapter 6

# Eternal Investing – Why We Give

A temporal worldview says, "It is more blessed
to keep than to give."

A biblical worldview says, "It is more blessed
to give than to receive."

*"In everything I did, I showed you that by this kind
of hard work we must help the weak, remembering
the words the Lord Jesus himself said: 'It is more
blessed to give than to receive.'"*

Acts 20:35

As I just reviewed, no matter what I accumulate
in investments and net worth here on earth, it will all
eventually burn up. However, Jesus made it very clear in
Matthew 6 that we can invest for eternity.

*"Do not store up for yourselves treasures on earth,
where moths and vermin destroy, and where thieves
break in and steal. But store up for yourselves
treasures in heaven, where moths and vermin do not
destroy, and where thieves do not break in and steal."*

Matthew 6:19–20

Author Randy Alcorn has written a great little book
called *The Treasure Principle*, and he sums it up with one

simple phrase: "You can't take it with you, but you can send it on ahead." He goes on to say, "Let me assume the role of 'eternal financial counselor' and offer this advice: choose your investments carefully; compare their rates of interest; consider their ultimate trustworthiness; and especially compare how they will be working for you a few million years from now."[64]

## ... We can invest for eternity.

Investing for eternity is important, but there can be a very real struggle between your flesh and your heart when it comes to giving. God's Word reveals four core reasons we should focus on our eternal investments while we are in our temporary homes.

## REASON #1: **OUR CREATOR IS A GIVER**

One of the most well-known verses to believers and non-believers is John 3:16. It still shows up at a lot of sporting events today. This scripture does a great job of revealing the heart of our Creator.

*"For God so loved the world that he gave his one and only Son, that whoever believes in him shall not perish but have eternal life."*

John 3:16

In the first section of this scripture, there is a pattern that is repeated in 2 Corinthians 9:7.

*Each of you should give what you have decided in your heart to give, not reluctantly or under compulsion, for God loves a cheerful giver.*

These verses reveal that in God's economy giving and love are connected. He "loved" the world so much that He "gave" His Son. He also "loves" a cheerful "giver." In addition, Genesis 1:27 reveals that God created us in His image. If God is a giver who loves, then He created us to be givers who love.

## ... In God's economy giving and love are connected.

God connects giving and love together very uniquely. This revelation gets lived through fatherhood when I experience the joy of giving gifts to my children. Christmas and birthdays became more joyful when I moved from receiver to giver. My greatest experience of love comes when I am in a posture of giving.

God gave the greatest gift He had to give in His Son. Before I was a father, I don't know if I understood the worth and significance of this gift. In Romans 5:7, Paul says, *"Very rarely will anyone die for a righteous person, though for a good person someone might possibly dare to die."* As a father, I can tell you this scripture has a deeper meaning. I *might* lay my own life down for *YOU*; however, I can guarantee there are *no* scenarios where I could ever imagine giving up the life of one of my children for *anyone*. Our God did that for us. Not only did He give up His Son for us, but He gave up His Son when we were His enemy.

As I reflect on this, I'm struck by the phrase, "I love to give." I realize as we understand our Father and how He created us, not only do "I love to give; I give to love."

## REASON #2: **IT'S A COMMAND**

Any time I see the word "command," I pay attention. If God commands us to do something, I typically hear clear teaching and instruction from spiritual leaders. Unfortunately, in a world designed to make people feel good and shy away from criticism, I have found many ministries are reluctant to teach commands, especially when they are in an area as taboo as money and finances.

I read the following verses over several times to make sure I was reading them correctly. Sure enough, I was. Paul wrote it clearly in 1 Timothy.

> **Command** *those who are rich in this present world not to be arrogant nor to put their hope in wealth, which is so uncertain, but to put their hope in God, who richly provides us with everything for our enjoyment.* **Command** *them to do good, to be rich in good deeds, and to be generous and willing to share. In this way they will lay up treasure for themselves as a*

*firm foundation for the coming age, so that they may
take hold of life that is truly life (emphasis added).*
1 Timothy 6:17–19

I'm often uncomfortable when I see a command,
but this scripture is very clear. I attempted to disqualify
myself by saying, "I'm not rich." Unfortunately, I was
quickly proven wrong. Remember back in Chapter 3
about planning for us? I presented data that shows if you
make more than $35,000 annually in the United States,
your income is higher than 99% of the rest of the world.
That certainly qualifies me (and most people I know) as
being rich.

God also commanded giving in Deuteronomy.

*Give generously to them and do so without a grudging
heart; then because of this the Lord your God will
bless you in all your work and in everything you put
to your hand to. There will always be poor people in
the land. Therefore I **command** you to be openhanded
toward your fellow Israelites who are poor and needy
in your land (emphasis added).*
Deuteronomy 15:10–11

God understands how much generosity affects our
attitudes toward others. What we often miss is that in
both of these passages there is a blessing and reward in
following these commands (more on that under Reason
#3). However, I often struggle with the lie of the Enemy
that tells me if I give something away, I will have less.

Gunnar Johnson is a pastor at Gateway Church in Southlake, Texas, and summed it up well when he said, "The reality of life is we can never have enough money to be secure, satisfied or feel significant."[65] My flesh will always desire more, so why not take God at His word and experience the blessing for myself.

If I'm going to obey the command of God to give, I have to start somewhere. Fortunately, God's Word speaks very plainly in this area. The Word of God reveals we are to Give First, Give Much and Give More than money.

## GIVE FIRST

*Honor the Lord with your possessions, and with the firstfruits of all your increase; so your barns will be filled with plenty, and your vats will overflow with new wine.*

Proverbs 3:9–10 (NKJV)

The firstfruits are the first of everything that comes in. The very first check Angel and I write every month is to giving.

In the process of doing this, we experienced one of God's miracles. When we were first giving early in our marriage, we would take care of all of our bills and then see what was left over to give. As you can imagine, most months there wasn't anything left. However, when Angel and I started giving first, we discovered we had more than enough to care for our family. Nothing changed about our income, but God was at work as we obeyed His commands.

Early in my Christian walk, I struggled with the story of Cain's and Abel's offerings. I didn't understand why God would find Abel's gift more favorable than Cain's. Both men were giving to God, why would one gift be more appealing? When I understood the importance of giving first, it became crystal clear.

> *In the course of time Cain brought some of the fruits of the soil as an offering to the Lord. And Abel also brought an offering—fat portions from some of the firstborn of his flock. The Lord looked with favor on Abel and his offering, but on Cain and his offering he did not look with favor. So Cain was very angry, and his face was downcast.*
>
> Genesis 4:3–5

Abel brought his gift from the *"firstborn of his flock,"* while *"In the course of time"* Cain brought *"some of the fruits of the soil."* Abel gave from his *"first."* The importance of giving **first** cannot be underestimated.

---

**The importance of giving first cannot be underestimated.**

## GIVE MUCH

In his book, *Mere Christianity*, CS Lewis says, "I do not believe one can settle how much we ought to give. I am afraid the only safe role is to give more than we can spare."[66] As much as I like this quote, I have found that I, like most people, want some instructions on how much I should be giving and where I should start. Fortunately, God's Word gives us direction in this area. The model we often see in the church and the Scriptures starts with a tithe. The definition of a tithe is a tenth. When Angel and I began our giving journey, this is where we started.

More important than the amount is the attitude of our giving.

*Each of you should give what you have decided in your heart to give, not reluctantly or under compulsion, for God loves a cheerful giver.*

2 Corinthians 9:7

In the next chapter, I want to spend some time talking about how we can have more joy in our giving, but for now I think it is important that we approach any giving with the right attitude. Ultimately, God wants our hearts; He doesn't need our money!

**Ultimately, God wants our hearts; He doesn't need our money!**

There have been many debates about whether or not the tithe still applies today. The dividing line is usually drawn between the law of the Old Testament versus the grace of the New Testament. Did Jesus do away with the law through grace or did He confirm the law? These debates lead to further disagreements that unfortunately often cause divisions in the Church. I'm not going to use this book to flesh out these positions. I will, however, share with you the one point of scripture and law that is very clear to me. Every time I see Jesus discussing the Jewish law, He ends up raising the standard.

Regarding murder, Jesus says:

*"You have heard that it was said to the people long ago, 'You shall not murder, and anyone who murders will be subject to judgment.' But I tell you that anyone who is angry with a brother or sister will be subject to judgment. Again, anyone who says to a brother or sister, 'Raca,' is answerable to the court. And anyone who says, 'You fool!' will be in danger of the fire of hell."*
Matthew 5:21–22

Regarding adultery, Jesus says:

*"You have heard that it was said, 'You shall not commit adultery.' But I tell you that anyone who looks at a woman lustfully has already committed adultery with her in his heart."*
Matthew 5:27–28

If Christ is raising the standard of the Jewish law in these areas, then why should we expect anything less in our giving? If the starting point of giving in the Old Testament law was a tenth, then it certainly seems that, at a minimum, we should start with a tenth and seek His guidance on what more He would have us give as our giving matures.

One of the most compelling scriptures in the Bible regarding giving is hidden in the last book of the Old Testament. This scripture has shaped my giving experience more than any other.

> *"Will a mere mortal rob God? Yet you rob me. But you ask, 'How are we robbing you?' In tithes and offerings. You are under a curse—your whole nation—because you are robbing me. Bring the whole tithe into the storehouse, that there may be food in my house. Test me in this," says the Lord Almighty, "and see if I will not throw open the floodgates of heaven and pour out so much blessing that there will not be room enough to store it."*

Malachi 3:8–10

It's easy to focus on the negative part of this scripture where God calls the people under a curse for withholding their giving; however, the most beautiful piece of this scripture sits in the last half of God's statement. God challenges us to test Him in our giving. Through this test, God wants to *"throw open the floodgates of heaven and pour out so much blessing."* This is the only place in God's Word where God says, *"Test me."* Angel and I have found this test is one that is worth taking, and as I have challenged other believers, I've never seen anyone disappointed with how that test turned out.

## GIVE MORE THAN MONEY

When I began my giving journey, I often only focused on the dollars I was giving. I've come to learn it is just as important to consider my time and talents as a portion of my giving.

> *Then Jesus said to his host, "When you give a luncheon or dinner, do not invite your friends, your brothers or sisters, your relatives, or your rich neighbors; if you do, they may invite you back and so you will be repaid. But when you give a banquet, invite the poor, the crippled, the lame, the blind, and you will be blessed. Although they cannot repay you, you will be repaid at the resurrection of the righteous."*
>
> Luke 14:12–14

I've since taken these scriptures as a challenge to look for opportunities to serve those who can't repay us. Our family found that volunteering in our community at a Food Bank gives us a different perspective on hunger and need. We also found going on mission trips is effective because it gets us out of our comfort zones and allows us to see and serve people where they live. I'm always careful not to limit my giving to my checkbook but to look for opportunities to get our family's heart and hands engaged in what is going on in the world.

---

### ... Look for opportunities to serve those who can't repay us.

---

## REASON #3: **THERE ARE TEMPORAL BENEFITS**

When I first began giving, my focus was on what I was giving up rather than what I was gaining. I discovered God has hardwired man to be a giver so strongly even our US Tax Code benefits givers.

In order to see the potential personal benefits in giving, you have to understand there are three forms of capital at work.

- Family Capital is the income and assets I have control over and direct today and throughout my lifetime.

- Taxable Capital is the portion of my income and assets that have to be given to the US government to provide for the greater social welfare of our citizens.

- Giving Capital is the portion of my income and assets I choose to direct to ministries and programs I see doing good work.

Most of us could acknowledge these forms of capital, but rarely ever think of how they might be related. The reason we have an incomplete understanding is that we are operating from two common misconceptions that limit our giving potential.

The first misconception is that "All of our Taxable Capital has to go to the IRS." Most people believe this to be true and rather than planning ahead, simply pay all of the income, capital gains and estate taxes to the IRS without any consideration of how they might be minimized or avoided.

The second misconception says, "If my family allocates Giving Capital to meet opportunities, then it decreases the amount of Family Capital available." We like giving to various causes, but we love our families more than we like someone's cause. Because of these misconceptions, most people give far less than they have potential.

Both of these misconceptions are common, but once you begin to understand them, they become a powerful ally. If you plan strategically, you can convert certain Taxable Capital to Giving Capital. The conversion of Taxable Capital to Giving Capital benefits your family and the ministries you support. Jesus stated very clearly that we should:

*"Give back to Caesar what is Caesar's ..."*
Matthew 22:21

However, I also believe we shouldn't give back more than we have to.

**Please Note:** There is a very big difference between tax avoidance and tax evasion. One can be done through strategic planning with good tax advisors and one leads straight to prison.

Here is the simplest of examples. The IRS will give you a tax deduction on your gifts to qualified ministries and non-profits. If you are in a 25% tax bracket and make a $1,000 gift, you will realize a tax savings of $250 for your gift; therefore, giving $1,000 only costs you $750.

I am not going to focus on all of the specific strategies in this book as their number and combinations could take up a book of their own. It is important to note through proper planning with a tax advisor, income taxes can likely be reduced, capital gains taxes can be managed and estate taxes can potentially be avoided. Many of the outcomes are beautiful because this conversion of Taxable Capital into Giving Capital can possibly generate more Family Capital to use and control.

Remember Bob and Janet, who we talked about in a previous chapter? They were preparing to sell their business. Instead, they were able to take a portion of the business and turn it into Giving Capital that could provide an increased income for them for the remainder of their lives. By doing this, the strategy they used allowed them to avoid any capital gains taxes on the sale of that portion of the business. Bob and Janet received a current tax deduction for making the gift they could use to reduce their current income taxes. This one idea turned some of their Taxable Capital into Family Capital and Giving Capital. They will be able to use this increased income for the rest of their lives, and when they pass away, they are leaving a gift to their church and some local ministries they support.

## Converting Taxable Capital into Giving Capital allows us to see God's economy at work.

Converting Taxable Capital into Giving Capital allows us to see God's economy at work. Read what Paul writes in 2 Corinthians 9:6, *"Remember this: Whoever sows sparingly will also reap sparingly, and whoever sows generously will also reap generously."* I was raised in West Texas, and many of the members of my family were farmers. Most of them farmed cotton. What did they get when they farmed cotton? Well, it would be strange if they received anything but cotton, wouldn't it? They didn't expect apples or oranges, they expected cotton.

I have observed the same laws at work in giving. When I sow finances, I've observed financial blessing flowing into my life. I'm not trying to present God as some type of genie or guarantee financial success when you give, but it is also hard to deny what I have observed in my life and the lives of others.

It is important to realize that some harvests take longer. There are different seasons for different types of crops, and I've noticed when it comes to finances certain harvest seasons change. However, one of the things I've noted is that most families' balance sheets seem to grow as they give and invest eternally. Stated differently, I've heard it said, "If God can get it through you, God will get it to you."[67]

Amazingly, I've never observed anyone going broke by giving money away. One of the best real world examples of this happened in the life of R.G. LeTourneau. He owned a business in the earthmoving equipment sector in the early 1900s, and he had a heart for giving. Throughout his life he continued to increase his giving until he was giving away 90 percent of his income and living on 10 percent. Even at this level of giving, his wealth continued to grow. When someone asked him how it happened, he said, "I shovel it out and God shovels it back in, but God has a bigger shovel."[68]

## REASON #4: **OUR GIVING WILL AFFECT OUR ETERNITY**

Through Scripture, we understand we will have to answer eternally for what we've done with what we've been entrusted with. Considering how important giving is to God, it makes logical sense that we will be judged on our giving.

In 2 Corinthians 5:10, Paul is writing to believers when he says, *"For we must all appear before the judgment seat of Christ, so that each of us may receive what is due for the things done while in the body, whether good or bad."* We know believers will not be judged for our salvation, but we will be judged for what we did with what we were given.

In 1 Corinthians, Paul writes about the importance God places on what I build for eternity while I am here on earth.

*If anyone builds on this foundation using gold, silver, costly stones, wood, hay or straw, their work will be shown for what it is, because the Day will bring it to light. It will be revealed with fire, and the fire will test the quality of each person's work. If what has been built survives, the builder will receive a reward. If it is burned up, the builder will suffer loss but yet will be saved—even though only as one escaping through the flames.*

1 Corinthians 3:12–15

If you read this passage carefully, you see there are believers who will make it into heaven, but based on how they stewarded their blessing, their clothes will be singed and smoky from barely escaping the testing of fire.

You may be familiar with the phrase, "There are no U-Hauls behind hearses."[69] If we acknowledge this is true, then why do we spend so much energy in our lives focusing on temporary endeavors? I pull out my investment account statements when they come in every month and want to know how my temporal investments have performed. Have I also put a conscious effort around the performance of my eternal investment account?

---

## In eternal investing, God never has a bear market.

---

Here is some great news: In eternal investing, God never has a bear market. As a matter of fact, in God's economy, the returns are phenomenal. How do I know this? Consider the examples that are all throughout the Bible: manna in the desert, the widow and the jars of oil, Jesus turns water to wine, Jesus feeds the five thousand (These are just a few of the numerous examples throughout Scripture).[70] If God can create those types of returns with our eternal investing, why wouldn't we want to put as much money as we can toward that endeavor?

In Matthew 25:21 we reach the end of the story of the Parable of the Talents and Jesus says, *"His master replied, 'Well done, good and faithful servant! You have been faithful with a few things; I will put you in charge of many things. Come and share your master's happiness!'"* My heart's desire is to one day hear God say, "Well done." We all want to be rewarded.

I once heard author, speaker, attorney and Honorary Consul for the Republic of Uganda, Bob Goff, speak, and he talked about the importance of praising other people. He has a habit of carrying little medals around with him to give out when he sees people doing something ordinary exceptionally well. I thought this was a great idea so I started carrying around some medals of my own. I soon realized the greatest place to start this recognition was with my own family. I spent the next month looking for opportunities to reward each one of my children with a medal.

---

## We simply need to keep our eyes on the eternal prize.

---

You should have seen how the eyes of my son Austen beamed when I awarded him a medal for following through on something he was afraid of. This is exactly what God wants to do for us. We are all His little kids, and when we get to heaven, God wants to give us a reward for how we managed the life He entrusted to us. We simply need to keep our eyes on the eternal prize.

---

- Does anything hold you back from giving?

- Do you believe it is possible to out-give God?

- What do we miss out on if we refuse to give?

- How does my giving help me to connect with God and His calling on my life?

---

# Chapter 7

# Eternal Investing – The Heart and Joy of Giving

A temporal worldview says, "Getting rich
and having more is my priority."

A biblical worldview says, " 'True Life' comes
from being generous."

*Command those who are rich in this present world
not to be arrogant nor to put their hope in wealth,
which is so uncertain, but to put their hope in God,
who richly provides us with everything for our
enjoyment. Command them to do good, to be rich in
good deeds, and to be generous and willing to share.
In this way they will lay up treasure for themselves
as a firm foundation for the coming age, so that they
may take hold of the life that is truly life.*

1 Timothy 6:17-19

I've noticed in my own nature a reluctance to give. It's
almost as if I'm afraid I may lose something if I give away
what I have. 1 Timothy 6:18 says, *"Command them to do
good, to be rich in good deeds, and to be generous and willing
to share."* My mind begins to think about all I might miss

out on if I am generous and willing to share. Too many times, I don't stop to realize the promise waiting one verse later in 1 Timothy 6:19: *"In this way they will lay up treasure for themselves as a firm foundation for the coming age, so that they may take hold of the life that is truly life."*

God actually wants me to experience "true life" through my giving?

*Each of you should give what you have decided in your heart to give, not reluctantly or under compulsion, for God loves a cheerful giver.*

2 Corinthians 9:7

As I began to think through my own giving, I wondered, *"Am I a cheerful giver? Do I know any cheerful givers?"* I began to wonder if something was broken in my giving, because I wasn't observing "true life" or "cheerfulness" when I gave.

As I grew up, the offering time at church was when they played somber music while people sat with their hands folded nicely in their laps as the offering plate was passed. I observed many people turning their heads as the plate passed in hopes that no one noticed they didn't give. As I got older, I noticed I often got uncomfortable when the preacher taught on giving. For some reason, I wasn't connecting to God's heart in the area of giving.

I began to understand this better during the 13-week course from Crown Financial I mentioned Angel and I had experienced early in our marriage. The first lesson from Crown taught us to be content with where God had placed us. I was never going to have true contentment if

I held on too tightly to everything I possessed. When I held on tightly to my possessions and time, nothing got out, but nothing could get in either. In Deuteronomy, God speaks directly against this:

> *If anyone is poor among your fellow Israelites in any of the towns of the land the Lord your God is giving you, do not be hardhearted or tightfisted toward them. Rather, be openhanded and freely lend them whatever they need.*
>
> Deuteronomy 15:7–8

I quickly realized I was living my life tightfisted. I needed to learn to live openhanded. Living with an open hand takes faith. When I am open, some of my possessions may escape, but I also leave myself in a position to receive more. Chip Ingram is a pastor and author in California, and I found his words sum up these thoughts well: "The only antidote I can find in the Scripture for greed and materialism is letting loose and giving what God has given you to help other people. If you do not release what God has entrusted to you, it will wrap its arms around your throat."[71]

---

## Living with an open hand takes faith.

---

Angel and I began to be open to giving a portion of ourselves away in money and time. Money was my greatest idol, and the only way to find freedom was to start giving financially. The Holy Spirit and scriptures convicted us that our financial giving should start at 10% of our income.

I didn't know what to expect, but God was up to something. Angel and I soon found out we were going to be parents with our first child, Clayton. We had always wanted her to stay home and raise our children rather than continue to work. As we sat down to do our budget, it became obvious we had a major issue. We cut our spending down to bare bones, and no matter how we looked at it, we were still $200 short every single month. It was through this dilemma my faith was truly stretched. If I chose not to give money away, we could meet our budget. If I gave the money away, we were short. Was I going to trust God and live openhanded, or was I going to close my fist and go back to doing it my way?

Remember Malachi 3:10, where God says, *"Test me in this?"* I realized God had placed us exactly where we needed to be, and this challenge was what we needed to face at that point in our lives. We decided to keep our commitment to giving, have Angel stay home and see what happened. The only rule we created was we would give away 10% of what we brought in, and no matter what, that was the first check we would write every month. On every one of these firstfruits checks, we would write "Thank You, God" on the "For" line of the check.

What happened? It was an amazing year. During that year, we kept our commitment to giving, paid off over $7,500 in debt and were never short on money. Within two years, I received a major promotion and moved to the New Orleans area. Not only had God revealed His faithfulness in our giving, He had stirred a passion and desire in us to discover how to be "cheerful" givers.

When you look more closely at the context of "cheerful," you gain greater insight into God's character. The word translated "cheerful" is the Greek word "*hilaros*" which is where we get the word hilarious. Think about when we use the word "hilarious." We use it when we are completely overcome by the joy in a situation. Can you imagine what things would look like if you went into a church or fundraiser where people were giving gifts and laughing out loud while they did it? You would think the people had lost their minds, yet this is the connection God is attempting to provide when we give.

One of the blessings of our giving journey is that God has helped us learn how to have joy in our giving. The process of discovering this joy came when I began to get connected with where my money was going. How many times did I make a gift and have no idea what it ultimately accomplished?

We made a decision to be intentional and take note if anything changed for us. At this time, we did not have a church home, so we had to be creative in how we looked for places to give. The easiest thing for us was to review offers we received in the mail. The requests came from various locations, but three that stick in my memory were a food bank, a women's shelter and a parenting center.

Angel and I would take each offer and pray for God to guide our giving. In many of these gifts, we knew exactly what the money was for. For example, when we gave to the food bank, we knew we were providing five to ten meals for someone. When we made a gift to the parenting center, they would use it to purchase diapers or a new high chair. Knowing what the money was for brought a brand new level of joy to our giving.

I've encouraged other givers who are struggling with getting excited about their giving to try the same thing. I encourage you to find somewhere you can see a direct impact and focus your giving there for a season. You might be amazed at your own attitude transformation.

This experience gave us a whole new perspective and allowed us to really enjoy what we were doing. We've continued this with a portion of our giving today and have shared this joy with our children, specifically through the organization Compassion International. Through Compassion, we sponsor kids who match each one of our children's ages. What has this done? It has allowed our children to see a real human being who's benefiting from their giving. They get to watch this child grow up. They get to communicate with them, and they get to share life with them. They also get to see that not everyone has the same blessings they have. The joy our children experience through these simple sponsorships has been immeasurable.

We are blessed by the teachings of our local church and are impressed with how they are reaching out to our local community. I've met people who say they are reluctant to give to the church because they aren't happy with how the church is using the funds. I believe the Scriptures very clearly state that our first portion of giving should go to our local church. Just as we are stewards, the church is called to be stewards of their funds. The more active we make ourselves in serving through the church body, the more we are able to stay connected to our giving. If your church giving feels disconnected, then I encourage you to find a place to serve and see if God doesn't change your heart. We have been blessed that the majority of churches we have attended have done a good job communicating the use of the tithes and offerings. However, if you do find yourself in a situation where, after all of this, you can't get comfortable with how the church is stewarding the tithes and offerings, then you may need to find a new church.

Beyond our church giving, we struggle with the needs we see in each and every new request. It appears when you give money to one organization, they share your name and address with others. We know we can't meet all of those needs. Do we send a really small amount to each one or would we be better off making a larger impact on a few organizations? Over time, God has led us to specific issues we are passionate about supporting.

---

**... "True life" and being "cheerful" in giving come easier when you are funding causes you can get excited about.**

---

We know there is much good to be done in the world, but we also know it's not our job to do it all. In our lives, the giving became so much easier when we found groups that met our passions. Today, we focus our giving on organizations that support families, take care of children and orphans and work to end child trafficking. We've found there is enough to be done in those areas that we could focus there for a lifetime, but we are also open to the fact God may lead us to other areas as we move through life. For you, there may be different issues you care about, but I would encourage you to realize that "true life" and being "cheerful" in giving come easier when you are funding causes you can get excited about.

As givers, we know it is important to know how our money is being used. It would be irresponsible if we simply gave money but didn't take the time to find out how effective our gifts were and how they were being applied. There are many great resources on the Internet that can help with this research. I believe CHARITYNAVIGATOR.ORG is a good tool for our family. Charity Navigator has a rating system that looks at: "Two broad areas of a charity's performance; their financial health and their accountability and transparency. (The) ratings show givers how efficiently (they) believe a charity will use their support today, how well it has sustained its programs and services over time and their level of commitment to good governance, best practices and openness with information."[72]

I know my tendency is to try to simplify the decision and simply look at the bottom line of how much money that is donated goes out to the programs that are being used. That certainly is one measure, but I found we might miss some incredible opportunities if we avoided making an investment because we observed an organization's overhead was too high. There are a number of wonderful organizations that have a high overhead because it costs that much to run the ministry programs that are providing value. When you can, it is valuable to visit with the organization you support. Every time we have requested this, the ministry has been excited to tell us their story. They've been honest and forthcoming about any issues or challenges we had observed in our research.

As we give more to specific ministries, we ask them to let us know how they plan to use the money. This becomes an opportunity to share our giving experience with our kids. Just like us, our kids get a real joy knowing the outcomes our giving provides and have many times added their own funds to the cause. The more involved we become, the more informed we become; and the more informed we become, the more engaged we become.

As our financial giving grew, I wondered if I was limiting our ability to experience the joy of giving. It is a lot easier to write a check than it is to get involved. When I send a check to someone, I can try to stay engaged with the organization, but no matter how much I attempt to keep up with things, I'm never going to get the full story unless I get personally involved. Paul even understood this when he was communicating to Timothy. Notice he says, *"Command them to do good, to be rich in good deeds."* There was that word again: "command." Not only did I need to look at how we were giving money, I needed to take a hard look at how we were giving our time.

---

### ... The joy of serving is almost always expressed best in groups.

---

As Angel and I prayed about how to live this out, God impressed upon us this needed to be a family affair. I also knew the joy of serving is almost always expressed best in groups. We created something we called a "Doing Good Day." I felt a lack of connectedness to our community, and as I looked around, it was obvious there were many great organizations doing tremendous work. We called various groups and looked specifically for organizations that would allow us to partner with them while we brought the kids along.

Painting various cones and barrels for future riding at the therapy center.

In our first project, we worked with a local therapeutic riding center that helps disabled children and war veterans through horseback riding. We went out and painted some of the barrels and fences for them and spent about half a day getting to know their work better. Our kids had a wonderful time.

For the next event, we worked with a local special needs facility painting their back fence in preparation for their summer programs.

My favorite memory from a Doing Good Day happened in September of 2014 when we were volunteering with a local food bank. The food bank

Painting the fence of the playground at the development center.

had a parking lot that desperately needed more gravel. It was me and four boys ranging from ages 9 to 13 who completed the job—shoveling and hauling gravel all over the parking lot. I've never seen boys work harder or more diligently than they

Students painting the murals on the completed fence at the development center.

did that day. It filled my heart with joy to know those boys were able to help while also realizing a sense of satisfaction in a job well done.

The kids will tell you their favorite Doing Good Day (DGD) happens every Labor Day weekend. We partner with a ministry out of Texas that helps free children from slavery in the fishing industry in Ghana, Africa.[73] Every Labor Day, our kids put on a bake sale to raise money for this ministry. They work to help bake the goods, package the goods, and we involve many of our friends and family in helping pull it all together. When it comes to the day of the event, the kids are in charge of selling all the goods and raising the money. Words can't express

Spreading gravel on the local food bank parking lot.

how exciting it is to see the smiles on their faces as they know the work they're doing is going for a greater cause. It's fulfilling to see their concern for the kids who are in Ghana and their genuine desire to participate, knowing how much good the money they raise can do.

---

## Once you have caught the spirit of giving, it's something you want to share.

---

These experiences have become contagious and allow our entire family to experience joy in our giving. When you mention to our kids that today is a DGD, it's almost as if you told them they were going to Disney World. It's hard to get our kids to clean up after themselves at home, but if you had seen them cleaning at a home for unwed mothers, you would have tried to hire them to come to your home and clean. Once you have caught the spirit of giving, it's something you want to share. We know one of us can only make a small difference, but all of us working together can be a true force for change.

During one of our Doing Good Days, the Volunteer Coordinator came up and asked, "What church is this?" I told her we were not "a church," but we were "the Church" in action. We are a group of believers being the hands and feet of Christ in our community. This isn't a movement of religion; this is a movement to serve like our Creator.

Today we have DOINGGOODDAYS.COM. My hope is that over time, the site will encourage others to create a day of their own and give back to their communities. Together, we can experience each other's joy and encourage one another. We might even find a new way to serve that we've never thought of before. There is power in a serving community.

In the summer of 2013, we felt called to make an impact with our family somewhere outside of our community. We needed to get outside of our comfort zone, and the only way Angel and I knew to do that was to take our entire family on a mission trip. In March of that year, we started talking to our kids about the possibility, and our daughter, Gracyn, said she wanted to go to Mexico, play with the little kids and give them lollipops and bubbles. We thought this was a nice gesture, but ignored the thought as we started looking for different ways to embrace this new opportunity.

We spent the next few months calling and looking at every mission opportunity we could find. Some of them were international; some of them were within the United States. At the time, Gracyn was 6, Austen was 9 and Clayton was 11. The challenge we ran into was that the minimum age to go on any mission trip with all of the organizations we talked to was 12. Clayton would be 12 before the summer rolled around, but our desire was for our entire family to serve together.

We continued to search and got our friends and church active in the search, as well. In May, we found a ministry located in San Diego, California, called Amor. Amor has spent the last 30 years going to the dumps of Tijuana and building homes for families in that area. What excited us the most is that the minimum age to go on a trip with Amor was three.

We found a place where our entire family could serve! (*It did not escape our notice that we were to serve in Mexico, the place Gracyn had said we should go all those months before.*) In order to get to San Diego, our family drove to save a little bit on cost. During the drive, we did everything a family could do from a tourist standpoint. We went to Carlsbad Caverns, the Grand Canyon and the Petrified Forest. We spent time at Disneyland. We went to LEGOLAND and the San Diego Zoo. We even went to the beach.

During the final three days of our trip, our family spent time down in Mexico working alongside other families with Amor, building a home for a family who happened to have a young daughter who was Gracyn's age.

Gracyn spent the days of our trip playing with

Fernanda and Gracyn playing with the bubbles Gracyn brought to give "the little girl of the house."

this little girl, and at the end, she gave her some bubbles, lollipops and some markers. Gracyn's vision was fulfilled, and our family was hooked. As we were getting on the bus to come home, Gracyn looked at me and said, "We're coming back next year, right?"

The true joy of this entire trip was formed in concrete after we came home. We had been gone for two and a half weeks and spent three days in Mexico. Yet, when anyone asked my children what they did that summer, their comment was, "We went to Mexico and built a house!" It was at that point I knew those three days had made all the difference.

We've returned to Mexico with Amor several times since then. One of the mottos of Amor is "disrupt." I think this trip does a good job of helping to disrupt our lives—and that is why we keep going back! I find my life is so comfortable that unless I get disrupted, I run the risk of getting complacent. Here are some thoughts I journaled after one of our trips:

Gracyn desperately tries to hit the nail on the head as we form up the walls on the first day.

You leave the US and cross the border into Mexico. Technically, you are only minutes from your home country, but you realize quickly you are not in control. Mexico just feels different. The minute I step into that country, my heart goes out to them. It feels very oppressive and helps me to appreciate the freedom we enjoy at home.

When we arrive at the camp, there is no electricity; there is no running water. You make your camp on the hard desert ground. The bathrooms are seats over a large trench. The showers are open air enclosures. You are reminded how well we have it at home. In addition, the pastors' wives who serve the meals and take care of the camp have some of the biggest smiles. The pastors who come to share their stories bring warmth to your soul on a cool night.

We head to the work site in an old school bus. The roads are not paved or well-maintained. The ride is hot and very bumpy. Yet, everyone we pass seems happy and content. You ask yourself, "How is that possible?" When we arrive at the work site, we meet the new family. We don't

Clayton, Austen, and Eric work to filter rocks from the sand in order to make the stucco for the outside of the house.

have power tools, just saws and hammers. The work is hard. We sweat in the hot July sun. I think to myself, "I don't know when I've had this much fun with my family!"

At the end of the day, we head back to camp. I notice something is missing ... the distractions. No one can call me here. I don't have Internet access, and my email doesn't work. There is a certain joy in this. We sit around the campfire, roast marshmallows and realize this trip isn't long enough. We will soon be going home. These disruptions are special, but unfortunately they wear off. When we return home, I find myself missing the disruption. I think of ways to create more disruption in my life. Typically, I think we all want to find our lives following a path that feels comfortable. We've found that comfortable is boring. Disruption brings joy, and I never want to forget that.

## Disruption brings joy and I never want to forget that.

As we have been experiencing this joy through missions, I continue to get one question I was not expecting. Angel and I will talk about our experience, the excitement of the kids over going back again, and when we invite a family to come with us, they often ask, "Is it safe?" The first time someone asked I was taken aback, but as I reflected on it, I realized this seems to be a default question in our culture today.

This question seems to be more and more prevalent over the last 10 years. I do know if my mom had asked that question with the consistency and urgency I often hear, it is unlikely I would have gone outside the house or played football with the neighbor kids.

While there are certainly times and places for an element of safety, I would argue that living with a strict definition of "safe" is boring. I actually can't remember the last time I had any fun being absolutely "safe." When I reflect on this idea, I realize Angel and I would not be where we are today if we had taken the "safe" route.

God calls us to be good stewards of everything we own, and I certainly take the stewardship of my family very seriously. However, at a certain point, we have to trust God's calling and Sovereignty in order to join Him in His great adventure. We partner with a wonderful organization that has been building homes in Mexico for the last 30 years. They've taken thousands of families on building trips into Mexico. They have canceled trips when the conditions weren't right. I trust our resources to take care of us. Most of all, I trust that if God has called us to go, then it doesn't matter if it's safe. I do know some of the best family memories we have, happened on these trips. I wouldn't trade that for anything.

Eric and Ramiro hug after a moving Key Ceremony when Ramiro was presented with keys to his new home. He took off work from a local t-shirt factory to help build his home.

## ... Being "recklessly faithful" to God's plan is fun, exciting and extremely rewarding

Perhaps this attitude is summed up best in a new term Angel recently coined for our family. She said our lives are to be lived "recklessly faithful." In the Scriptures, Jesus never called us to live lives of safety; He actually called us to something quite the opposite. I would encourage you to consider where you might be looking for safety in your life and examine if that is the right decision. From our own personal experience, I would tell you that being "recklessly faithful" to God's plan is fun, exciting and extremely rewarding!

The entire group who built Ramiro, Daniela and Fernanda's house. Most of us did not know one another before, but we have built several houses together since. We came from Louisiana, Indiana, California and Tennessee.

I know you may be overwhelmed by what needs to be done. Understand this: You can't do everything, but you can do something. God is calling you to this great adventure. He has designed each one of us uniquely. Start with the passions and callings God has placed on your heart. Start small, but definitely start!

- When was the last time you experienced joy in giving time, talents or money?

- Would you like to experience this joy again? How could you do that?

- What small step could you take today that could give you greater connection to your giving?

# Final Thoughts

We began our journey together by asking a simple question, "What if we've been doing it all wrong?" I grew up hearing the phrase, "If you find yourself in a hole, the first thing to do is stop digging." Both phrases reflect the idea we should stop what we are doing and consider taking another path. God is inviting us to "take hold of life that is truly life." His principles have not changed, but the world is fighting against them. I invite you to take these ideas and apply them to your life. The drastic amount of change God has woven through our lives because of them has been incredible. Following God's ideals won't necessarily be easy. Some of your friends may not understand, but I promise, you won't regret it!

# ENDNOTES

## INTRODUCTION

[1]"Worldview." American Heritage® Dictionary of the English Language, Fifth Edition. 2011. Houghton Mifflin Harcourt Publishing Company 29 Mar. 2016 http://www.thefreedictionary.com/worldview

[2]Tackett, Del. "What's Your View of the World?" *Focus on the Family.* N.p., n.d. Web. Apr. 2014

[3]Tackett, Del. "What's Your View of the World?" *Focus on the Family.* N.p., n.d. Web. Apr. 2014

[4]Tackett, Del. "What's Your View of the World?" *Focus on the Family.* N.p., n.d. Web. Apr. 2014

[5]"Barna Survey Examines Changes in Worldview Among Christians over the Past 13 Years." *Barna.* The Barna Group, Ltd., 9 Mar. 2009. Web. Apr. 2014.

[6]Tackett, Del. "What's Your View of the World?" *Focus on the Family.* N.p., n.d. Web. Apr. 2014

[7]Matthew 12:3, 5; Matthew 19:4; Matthew 22:31 (NKJV)

## CHAPTER 1: UNDERSTANDING WORLDVIEW

[8]Psalm 139:14

[9]Moore, T. M. "How the Money Changes Hands." *A Chuck Colson Center ViewPoint Study* (2009): 13. BreakPoint. Web. Apr. 2014.

[10]Moore, T. M. "How the Money Changes Hands." *A Chuck Colson Center ViewPoint Study* (2009): 11. BreakPoint. Web. Apr. 2014.

[11]Moore, T. M. "How the Money Changes Hands." *A Chuck Colson Center ViewPoint Study* (2009): 11. BreakPoint. Web. Apr. 2014.

[12]Moore, T. M. "How the Money Changes Hands." *A Chuck Colson Center ViewPoint Study* (2009): 13. BreakPoint. Web. Apr. 2014.

[13]Psalm 4:7

[14]Moore, T. M. "How the Money Changes Hands." *A Chuck Colson Center ViewPoint Study* (2009): 10. BreakPoint. Web. Apr. 2014.

[15]Deuteronomy 8:18

[16]1 Chronicles 29:11

[17]Moore, T. M. "How the Money Changes Hands." *A Chuck Colson Center ViewPoint Study* (2009): 17. BreakPoint. Web. Apr. 2014.

## CHAPTER 2: UNDERSTANDING STEWARDSHIP

[18]Moore, T. M. "How the Money Changes Hands." *A Chuck Colson Center ViewPoint Study* (2009): 17. BreakPoint. Web. Apr. 2014.

[19]"Steward." *Dictionary.com Unabridged.* Random House, Inc. 29 Mar. 2016. <Dictionary.com http://www.dictionary.com/browse/steward>.

[20]Link, E.G. "Jay" *Spiritual Thoughts on Material Things.* N.p.: Xulon, 2009. Print.

[21]Link, E.G. "Jay" "Keeping the Heart of God at the Heart of Living." *Who's in Charge Here?* Mooresville: Stewardship Ministries, 2013. 12. Print.

## CHAPTER 3: WHAT IF WE'VE BEEN DOING IT ALL WRONG IN PLANNING FOR US?

[22]globalrichlist.com

[23]Howard Dayton founded Crown Ministries in 1985. In 2000, Crown merged with Larry Burkett's Christian Financial Concepts to form Crown Financial Ministries. In 2007, Howard left his role as CEO at Crown. In 2009, he founded a new financial ministry: Compass—finances God's way. Although the teaching at Crown Financial is still much the same, Howard's departure has led to certain changes in the curriculum. Crown Financial is not affiliated with, nor endorsed by LPL Financial.

[24]Blue, Ron. *Master Your Money: A Step-by-step Plan for Gaining and Enjoying Financial Freedom.* Chicago, IL: Moody Publishers, 2004. 68. Print.

[25]Weisman, Mary-Lou. "The History of Retirement from Early Man to AARP." *New York Times* (March 21, 1999): n. pag. Print.

[26]Staff, Seattle Times. "A Brief History of Retirement: It's a Modern Idea." *The Seattle Times* 31 Dec. 2013, Local Politics ed., Nation & World sec.: n. pag. Web. Apr. 2014.

[27]This quote was used by Jay Link in an email where he announced he was retiring from his career.

## CHAPTER 4: WHAT IF WE'VE BEEN DOING IT ALL WRONG IN PLANNING FOR OUR HEIRS?

[28]Alcorn, Randy. "Should We Leave Our Children Inheritances?" Web log post. *epm.org.* N.p., 12 Jan. 2015. Web. May 2015.

[29]Link, E.G. "Jay" "When You Give, You Will Take Away." Web log post. *Life Stewardship Newsletter.* Stewardship Ministries, n.d. Web. May 2015.

[30]Blue, Ron. "Your Transfer Decision." *Splitting Heirs.* Chicago: Northfield, 2004. 70. Print.

[31]Baris, Mitchell; Carla Garrity; Carol Warnick and John Warnick. "Maturity Markers: A New Paradigm for Trust Distribution Models and Gifting Strategies." *Family Firm Institute* (04 Oct. 2008): n. pag. Web. May 2015

[32]Deuteronomy 21:17

[33]Numbers 27:1–11

34Matthew 25:14–30 (NKJV)

35Blue, Ron. "Your Treatment Decision." *Splitting Heirs*. Chicago: Northfield, 2004. 82–83. Print.

36O'Neill, Jessie H. *The Golden Ghetto: The Psychology of Affluence*. Center City, MN: Hazelden, 1997. Print.

# CHAPTER 5: WHAT IF OUR FINANCIAL INVESTING IS TEMPORARY?

37Brumley, Albert Edward. *This World Is Not My Home*. Hymn.

38Kelly, David P. "Bear Markets and Subsequent Bull Runs." *JP Morgan Guide to the Markets*® 1Q 2016 (December 31, 2015): 14. Print.

39Dimensional Fund Advisors "Annualized Rates of Return (%)." *Matrix Book 2016: Historical Returns Data – US Dollars* (March 2016): 10. Print.

40The S&P 500 is widely regarded as the best single gauge of large-cap U.S. equities. There is over USD 7.8 trillion benchmarked to the index, with index assets comprising approximately USD 2.2 trillion of this total. The index includes 500 leading companies and captures approximately 80% coverage of available market capitalization.

41evalueator.com; briinstitute.com

42Information from evalueator.com.

43Siverling, John. "A Research Study on CIF Member Funds Composite Performance Relative to Industry Averages." *Christian Investment Forum*. N.p., May 2015. Web. <christianinvestmentforum.org>.

44Leonard, Howard "Rusty." "When Screening Investments for Christian Values, Does Sin Win?" *Stewardship Partners*. N.p., Dec. 2015. Web. <http://www.stewardshippartners.com/backtest.pdf>. Dimensional Fund Advisors "Annualized Rates of Return (%)." Matrix Book 2016: *Historical Returns Data – US Dollars* (March 2016): 10. Print.

Small companies are measured by the Russell 2000 Index®. The Russell 2000 Index® measures the performance of the 2,000 smallest companies in the Russell 3000.

Large companies are measured by the S&P 500. The S&P 500 Index is widely regarded as the best single gauge of the U.S. equities market. The index includes a representative sample of 500 leading companies in the leading industries of the U.S. economy. Bonds are measured by the Barclays US Corporate Investment Grade Index. This is an unmanaged index consisting of publicly issued US Corporate and specified foreign debentures and secured notes that are rated investment grade (Baa3/BBB or higher) by at least two ratings agencies, have at least one year to final maturity and have at least $250 million par amount outstanding. To qualify, bonds must be SEC-registered. All indices are unmanaged and may not be invested into directly.

45"Risk." *Dictionary.com* Unabridged. Random House, Inc. 24 Apr. 2016. <Dictionary.com http://www.dictionary.com/browse/risk>.

46"Who Is 'Harry Markowitz'" *Investopedia*. N.p., n.d. Web. Jan. 2016. <http://www.investopedia.com/terms/h/harrymarkowitz.asp>.

47"Volatility." *Dictionary.com* Unabridged. Random House, Inc. 26 Apr. 2016. <Dictionary.com http://www.dictionary.com/browse/volatility>.

48Kelly, David P. "Asset Class Returns." *JP Morgan Guide to the Markets*® 1Q 2016 (December 31, 2015): 59. Print.

49See #48 above for historical returns of stocks versus bonds.

50"The Prize in Economics 1990 – Press Release." Nobelprize. org. Nobel Media AB 2014. Web. 27 Apr 2016. http://www. nobelprize.org/nobel  prizes/economic-sciences/laureates/1990/ press.html

51"What is a Bear Market" *Investopedia*. N.p., n.d. Web. Jan. 2016. <http:// www.investopedia.com/terms/b/bearmarket.asp>. For purposes of this book, I include losses of 19% in a bear market. Although a loss of 19% does not technically cross the 20% threshold, most investors experience the same pain of loss during these periods as if they were bear markets.

52The S&P 500 Index is widely regarded as the best single gauge of the U.S. equities market. The index includes a representative sample of 500 leading companies in the leading industries of the U.S. economy. The S&P 500 Index focuses on the large-cap segment of the market; however, since it includes a significant portion of the total value of the market, it also represents the market. All indices are unmanaged and may not be invested into directly. This example includes three losses of 19% which occurred from 7/16/1990–10/11/1990, 7/17/1998–8/31/1998 and 4/29/2011–10/3/2011.

53Kelly, David P. "Annual Returns and Intra-Year Declines." *JP Morgan Guide to the Markets*® 1Q 2016 (December 31, 2015): 10. Print.

54Kelly, David P. "Bear Markets and Subsequent Bull Runs." *JP Morgan Guide to the Markets*® 1Q 2016 (December 31, 2015): 14. Print. In addition, there were three losses of 19% which occurred from 7/16/1990–10/11/1990, 7/17/1998–8/31/1998 and 4/29/2011–10/3/2011.

55The S&P 500 dropped 19% from a high of 1363.6 on 4/29/2011. It bottomed at 1099.2 on 10/3/2011. On 2/23/2012 the market traded over 1364.

56Swedroe, Larry. "The Smartest Things Ever Said About Market Timing." CBS News. *Moneywatch*, 25 Dec. 2009. Web. <http:// www.cbsnews.com/news/the-smartest-things-ever-said-about- market-timing/>.

57"S&P 500 Historical Prices by Year." *S&P 500 Historical Prices By Year*. N.p., n.d. Web. 01 May 2016. <http://www.multpl.com/s-p- 500-historical-prices/table/by-year>.

58This performance was calculated using a Hewlett Packard 10bii financial calculator using annual compounding.

59Kelly, David P. "Asset Class Returns." *JP Morgan Guide to the Markets*® 1Q 2016 (December 31, 2015): 59. Print.

[60]I was introduced to this phrase by author Nick Murray; however, I do not believe it is original to him. Unfortunately, during my research, I was unable to find the original author of this quote.

[61]Kelly, David P. "S&P 500 Index at Inflection Points." *JP Morgan Guide to the Markets*® 1Q 2016 (December 31, 2015): 63. Print.

[62]Poston, Toby. "The Legacy of JK Galbraith." *BBC News*. BBC, 30 Apr. 2006. Web. 01 May 2016. <http://news.bbc.co.uk/2/hi/business/4960280.stm>.

[63]Kelly, David P. "Diversification and the Average Investor." *JP Morgan Guide to the Markets*® 1Q 2016 (December 31, 2015): 63. Print.

## CHAPTER 6: ETERNAL INVESTING—WHY WE GIVE

[64]Alcorn, Randy. "Buried Treasure." *The Treasure Principle*. New York: WaterBrook Multnomah, 2001. 18–19. Print.

[65]Johnson, Gunnar. "Living a Blessed Life." *Generous Life Journey: The Road to Financial Freedom*. Grapevine: Gateway Create, 2013. 12. Print.

[66]Lewis, C. S. *Mere Christianity: Comprising the Case for Christianity, Christian Behaviour, and Beyond Personality*. New York: Touchstone, 1996. 82–83. Print.

[67]I have heard this quote many places, but it appears to originate with Andrew Wommack, a pastor in Colorado Springs, CO.

[68]LeTourneau, R. G. R.G. LeTourneau: Mover of Men and Mountains. Chicago: Moody, 1967. Print.

[69]Piper, John.

[70]Exodus 16, 2 Kings 4:1–7, John 2:1–12, Matthew 14:13–18

## CHAPTER 7: ETERNAL INVESTING—THE HEART AND JOY OF GIVING

[71]"Why God Prospers Generous People, Part 1." Interview by Chip Ingram. *Living on the Edge*. Suwanee, GA, 2010. Radio. Transcript.

[72]"How Do We Rate Charities?" *Charity Navigator*. N.p., n.d. Web. Mar. 2016. <charitynavigator.org>.

[73]For more information on this ministry, visit mercyproject.net.

# About the Author

Eric Dunavant was raised in a small town outside of Lubbock, Texas. His dad was a small-town veterinarian, and his mom stayed at home to raise Eric and his younger sister. Little did anyone know that Eric's mom would unexpectedly pass away when Eric was 14 years old. This left everyone in his family in disarray and set a trajectory for the journey of this book.

Eric went to school at Texas A&M University where he met the love of his life, Angel Linder Dunavant. They married in 1996, and God began to move in their lives shortly thereafter. *What If We've Been Doing It All Wrong?* is the story of a family seeking the Heart of God. Eric and Angel have been living a "Recklessly Faithful" life in Southeast Louisiana since 2003. They are the parents of Clayton, Austen and Gracyn. Together, their family is striving to glorify Christ, make disciples and maximize their impact on the Kingdom.

When Eric is not "ON," he can usually be found reading, doing *CrossFit* or watching Aggie sports, all while focusing on spending time enjoying his family.

If you would like to visit with Eric about speaking at your next event visit:

ericdunavant.com
or call
985-727-0770